A Prescription for Faith

Jose A. Caceres, MD

Print ISBN: 978-1-09835-202-8
eBook ISBN: 978-1-09835-203-5

Faith is God's work within us.

— *Thomas Aquinas*

Affectionately dedicated to my wife, Fe,

and

my sons, Joseph and Steven

Contents

Foreword

As a newly-ordained priest, my first years were filled with the blessing of preparing many couples for their weddings and then celebrating their wedding Masses. One such couple that particularly impressed me was Dr. Jose and Fe. They were different from many other couples who just wanted to focus on the wedding day. Jose and Fe wanted to focus on their marriage and were engaged in making sure they would be the best spouses to and for one another. They had a maturity, love, and faith that was not as present in many other couples, so I looked forward to our conversations as we explored how to ensure they would have a lifetime of love, fidelity and faith. After their wedding, when I had the opportunity to visit them in their office and eventually meet their two sons, I saw this love, care, and humble service continue to be shared with more and more people. So, it is my honor to briefly introduce Dr. Caceres to you.

Growing up in his native Peru, Dr. Caceres was blessed to have the seed of faith instilled in him at the beginning of his life. Baptism planted that seed, and his family cultivated and nourished that living faith. His expression of faith was made manifest in his desire to serve others, even at an early age. As his faith grew, his desire to express that faith became even stronger. Through prayer and discernment, Dr. Caceres came to know that his vocation was to be a medical doctor.

We all have had experiences with medical doctors at one time or another. The vast majority of us experience doctors during rushed office visits limited to discussing our medical issue of that present moment. In "A Prescription for Faith" Dr. Caceres, gives the reader an inside look at his vocation as a doctor and how much his faith plays an important role in his medical practice. In the call of Jesus for each of us to go out and make disciples of all nations (Mt 28:18-19), Dr. Caceres has shown us that one need not go off to a developing country to share Christ with others or have a theological degree, but that we can do it in our own daily lives. He is able, with great joy, to share the Catholic Christian faith that he has received.

Too many of us have tried to separate God from the many different aspects of our lives. This compartmentalization has led many to believe that God does not belong in our places of work. With his vision of faith and service in the workplace, Dr. Caceres shows the reader how he experiences and shares his faith in Christ in his daily work. An important factor in being able to do this begins with Dr. Caceres himself. He makes this quite clear. God has blessed him with a profound faith and that gift of faith cannot be kept to himself. It must be shared with others. Dr. Caceres is able to share his faith though patience, care, love, and above all the ability to see Christ in others. He makes it a point to look beyond a person's physical malady, emotional distress, and even religious persuasions (or lack thereof) to see and encounter Christ in all of his patients. In doing so, the door is opened for him to share the faith he so values in his life.

From the beginning of this book to the end, Dr. Caceres provides each of us with a framework for our lives, no matter what our vocation. He has a great love in his heart for all people, but especially for those who no longer practice their faith or who have never been given the opportunity to believe. Such people make up a sadly an ever-growing group in our country, and they deserve our attention. They deserve our very best efforts. Being able to share the faith with everyone we encounter, whether at work or play, is the root of us being able to serve our fellow man.

Most Revered Timothy Freyer, D.D.

Auxiliary Bishop

Diocese of Orange in California

November 2020

Acknowledgments

I extend to the Holy Trinity my sincerest gratitude for the gift of my Catholic faith. I give my heartfelt thanksgiving for the merciful love, blessings, and graces bestowed on me to become the person I am today: no more and no less to the eyes of God. Indeed, I wrote this book to the greater glory of God, so we can recognize our Lord in the faces and lives of the people we encounter every day.

To the Blessed Virgin Mary, Mother of Jesus, to whom I consecrated my entire self as a teenager.

My deepest gratitude to my lovely wife, Fe Caceres, for her unconditional love and patience with me as I devoted countless weekends to the preparation of this book, over the past three years.

My heartfelt appreciation to Pope Francis, who has inspired me to find God in all things, grow in my faith, persevere in prayer, and write this book centered on Jesus.

Special thanks to my patients for the privilege of serving as their physician, and for allowing me to share their stories in this work. I am truly grateful to these generous men and women and their families for welcoming me into their homes to record detailed accounts of their lives, including their joys and sorrows.

I am indebted to Derek Yee, my dearest and most loyal friend, who always was there for me, believed in me, supported me, and hoped for the best for me. He helped me to put one word after another, from A to Z, until the book was done. Truly, this book would not have materialized without his assistance.

Thanks to my colleagues and friends at the National University of Trujillo, School of Medicine, Class XII-1976, for their inspiration and encouragement to become a caring physician.

I extend my appreciation to Ninous Poureshagh, my friend and Chief Financial Officer at Caceres Medical Group, for his timely advice, assistance, and constant motivation to steadily grow our medical practice.

Thanks to my coworkers and staff at Buena Park Heart Center for helping me to provide medical services with a genuine caring attitude for more than 27 years.

My sincerest gratitude to Most Reverend Timothy Edward Freyer, Auxiliary Bishop, Diocese of Orange, California, for his invaluable time and dedication reviewing the manuscript for this work and generously writing its Foreword.

My warmest appreciation to the people who took the time to read and review this book before publication. Special thanks to Professor Peter Kreeft. I am also grateful to my colleagues Dr. Daniel Camarillo, Dr. Michael Shepard, and Dr. Daniel Valentini. Thanks also to Gary Abel, Steve Ezell, Vaughan Herrick, Emilie Kua, Julie Vetica, and Thomas Yee.

To Fr. Ed Broom, Fr. Larry Darnell, Fr. Craig MacMahon, Fr. Patrick Moses, and Fr. David Yankauskas I extend my deepest thanks for their significant contributions to my friendship with Jesus, steadfast encouragement, and kind reviews of this written work.

My gratitude to the priests and parishioners at St. Peter Chanel Catholic Church, St. Irenaeus Catholic Church, St. Hedwig Catholic Church, and St. Pius V Catholic Church, for their fellowship and support in worshipping and serving the Lord.

Finally, I thank you—the reader—for evaluating this book with an open mind and heart. It is my fondest wish that you will find words of reassurance in your faith and love for the Lord and our brethren in its pages.

Prologue

"Why do you still do it?" As a cardiologist with some 40 years in practice behind me now, I find that as the years tick on, I'm asked this question with ever-increasing frequency by the people closest to me. And as a man of 72 years of age, I'm sure the question of *how* I do it also features prominently in their minds. The latter I would attribute to the grace of God. As for the former—that is, why I have not yet retired to life of leisure in a quiet island paradise—well, to answer that, I must first take you back to a paradise of a different sort, the paradise of my childhood, my hometown of Trujillo, Peru.

My entry into this world was far from paradisiacal. I was born out of wedlock, and two months premature. The year was 1947, and specialized care for preterm babies was all but nonexistent, rendering my chances of survival very slim. But it would seem that God had other plans for me, as I not only survived, but later thrived in a large family of nine siblings.

My father, Antonio, was a hardworking man, the proprietor of a general merchandise store and candle factory that supported our family. Stern and demanding, but loving in his own way, he would abide neither disobedience nor laziness in his children. My mother, Celia, was a homemaker, understated yet strong, and endlessly supportive of her husband and nine children. To list the lessons I learned from these two dedicated dynamos would require a book unto itself. Papa Antonio and Mama Celia instilled in me and my eight sisters values and traditions that have quite literally lasted lifetimes.

At the core of these values lay the strong Catholic faith with which we were reared. From the start of my life, I was raised and bathed in the eternal tenets of the Catholic church, forming a relationship with God, attending mass, praying, and giving help to those in need. My father was a rector of the Cursillo de Cristiandad, and co-founder of an organization called Save our Lives, which found a family in need each week, and collected donations on their behalf. I have fond memories of visiting the homes of donors to gather food and clothing to deliver to struggling families. This helped me to identify in myself at an early age a strong desire to serve the needy. I also felt a growing desire to become more involved with the church as I grew older.

By the time I was ready to graduate from high school, my relationship with God had grown considerably. So, too, had grown my activities within the church and my yearning to help those in need. Thus, it seemed only natural that I should enter the priesthood. I sought the counsel of my father, who gave me his blessing to pursue the vocation, with the caveat that I must truly become a proper priest: I must carefully consider all that the profession entails, and be resolute in my conviction to make the necessary sacrifices. I took this advice to heart, and had an honest conversation with myself. The vows of poverty and obedience would be no trouble, I surmised, but the vow of chastity was another matter. In the end, my dream of one day starting a family led to my abandoning the notion of taking holy vows. What I would not—and indeed could not—abandon, however, was the intense yearning within me to serve.

If not as a priest, how, then, might I devote myself to helping those in need? There seemed only one clear choice: I would become a doctor. I would learn to cure the sick, to relieve pain and suffering, to minister to my brothers and sisters in Christ as an agent of healing and compassion. I considered my father's advice once more, this time as a prospective physician. *Would I be a proper doctor? Was I prepared to make the necessary sacrifices?* I answered the questions without hesitation, and so I set out to study medicine.

In the pages that follow, you will learn about my journey in the field of medicine, from my education and my earliest years in the profession to the current day. More importantly, you will read about the lives of some of the countless fascinating patients I have had the privilege of treating over the years. These will be true accounts, not embellished in any way, with only the names of the patients changed, to preserve their anonymity. You will read of good times and bad times, sorrows and joys. I hope to give you a glimpse into the sides of medicine of which, perhaps, only doctors are aware.

One common thread will tie together all of our stories—one that extends far beyond the limits of medicine and touches down on the very foundation of our being: faith. You see, the very faith that drew me to a life of service has continued to inform every aspect of my life, both in and out of the examination room. It has guided me in my moments of doubt, tempered me in my moments of frustration, helped me to heal in my moments of grief, and above all, allowed me to perform in my fullest capacity as a doctor to my patients. I say with conviction that my Catholic faith has been a steadfast and indispensable asset to me, not merely in my 40 years as a doctor, but in my 72 years as a human.

That is why I still do it.

Homelessness

My childhood home in Trujillo, Peru was sufficiently large for my parents and their eight energetic children. At the center of it lay a spacious rectangular patio from which the rest of the house branched out—bedrooms to the east and west, a living room to the north, and the kitchen and dining room to the south. It was on this patio that I would proudly learn to ride a bike, after falling countless times. On the street in front of the house, I would practice soccer— my favorite sport—with friends after school and on Saturdays. For many years, my sisters and I would play volleyball and find other ways to entertain ourselves on the grounds of this wonderful house, without a care in the world, and unaware of just how fortunate we were to have a place to call home.

For some, the matter of having a roof over their head is not a given. Over the last 25 years, in fact, I have seen a growing number of homeless people in the areas surrounding my practice. At the time of this writing in 2019, the homeless population in Orange County, California sits at a record high of 7,000, up from roughly 4,800 only two years ago. I was shocked to learn that veterans and seniors comprise more than half of this unfortunate community, some of whose members are my patients.

I think now of *Dorothy*, whose case illustrates some of the complexities faced by patients who lack permanent housing.

Born in 1961, Dorothy was the only girl in a family of three siblings. Her younger brother, Jim, had a congenital bone disease, which required multiple surgeries in his arms and legs from the time he was a toddler. As the years carried on, Jim's father served as an important source of inspiration to his sick child, encouraging the boy to walk, even though this caused him agonizing pain. Dorothy would watch these heart-wrenching scenes play out, unbeknownst to her father and brother, and cry silently in the wake of Jim's misery.

Dorothy began smoking at the age of 14, and took up alcohol a short time later. As a young adult, she would go on to attend for a time, stopping short of graduating. She became a single mother with two boys.

By the time Dorothy paid her first visit to my office, she was 40 years old, and her cigarette consumption had skyrocketed to 30 per day. Her alcohol consumption, too, had steadily progressed over the years, and she had become, in her own words, a "functional alcoholic."

Dorothy came to me with a long list of medical conditions, including anxiety, depression, bipolar disorder, obesity, hypertension, hyperlipidemia, thyroid disorders, chronic obstructive lung disease, neck injuries, and sciatica. She was seeing a psychiatrist for her anxiety and depression, and was taking multiple medications, most of which were for her mental illnesses. She was unable to hold a job, and used to sleep up to 15 hours per day. She became disabled following a neck surgery, and had also developed a heart condition.

Dorothy was living with an alcoholic boyfriend, and in spite of her failing health, she continued to smoke and drink for some time. Then one day, following a rift in the relationship, Dorothy realized she was tired of the problems her drinking had caused her, and she resolved to give it up entirely. She quit that very night, and has been sober for more than seven years since.

Following her breakup, Dorothy went on to live with her younger son and his wife, but this was to be short-lived, as she did not get along well with her daughter-in-law, and removed herself from the home shortly after her 52nd birthday.

Dorothy found herself with no place to go, and no money to pay for an apartment or even an inexpensive motel room. Her only recourse lay in her 1988 GM vehicle, which was to become her new home, stationed in a nearby city park. This abrupt change was very difficult for her in the beginning, but she adapted gradually to her new lifestyle. The park restrooms were open from 8 a.m. to 9 p.m. Outside of those hours, Dorothy was forced to postpone urination and bowel movements, sometimes to great discomfort. In the most extreme cases, e.g., when she suffered from loose stools, Dorothy was forced to employ diapers. She was the only woman among 25 to 30 other homeless people living in the vicinity of the park, and among the few who were not substance abusers.

From the beginning of Dorothy's homelessness, kind neighbors who lived nearby her parking spot offered her food and a place to take a shower when she wished to do so. Dorothy was reluctant to knock on their doors to solicit their assistance, though, as she did not want to impose. This led her to seek less invasive alternatives, such as enrolling in a local gymnasium, where, for ten dollars a month, she would have daily access to the showers.

At present, Dorothy's mobile phone is the only way she is able to communicate with the outside world, stay up on the news, keep appointments with her doctors, and talk to friends and relatives. She uses extra blankets to keep warm on cold and rainy nights. In spite of all her hardships, however, Dorothy considers herself fortunate, as she has her car for shelter—a relative luxury among the transient individuals with whom she shares the park.

Dorothy has tried to make use of different shelters, food banks, soup kitchens, and other places designed to help the homeless, but none of them has been able to offer a long-term solution to her problems. She cannot rent a P.O. Box, since local and federal government agencies require a street address for mail forwarding. As a result, Dorothy's small social security checks are mailed to the residence of her youngest son, whom she sees infrequently. This is an inefficient system, as she cannot retrieve her mail in a timely manner. It is not uncommon for large stacks of sometimes vital mail to be waiting for her. The gravity of this was highlighted in her recent failure to respond to a jury duty summons.

Dorothy does not eat regular hot meals, instead eating whatever is available at any given moment. On rare occasions, she will treat herself to a hamburger from one of the local fast food restaurants. Her 12 medications, by contrast, are handled much more predictably, as she diligently takes them throughout the day, as prescribed.

Dorothy sees her mission as being a helper to other homeless people in the park. Indeed, young and old alcohol- and drug-addicted outcasts come to her because she listens to them without passing judgment. Sometimes these individuals just want to talk to Dorothy, to get advice from her, or trust some of their belongings to her for a couple of hours. Unfortunately, Dorothy reports that many of them frequently steal to buy alcohol or drugs for personal use or resale.

An avid reader, Dorothy passes time by reading books in a variety of genres. Often, in an otherwise dark parking lot, one faint light can be seen shining from the front seat of a 31-year-old GM, as Dorothy reads the Holy Bible with the help of a flashlight.

Some time ago, the brakes on Dorothy's vehicle became faulty, and it could no longer be driven safely. She did not share this problem to us, but her uncharacteristic missing of medical appointments and treatments made it clear to us that something was amiss. Thankfully, a Good Samaritan provided her with the money to replace her brakes. When later Dorothy's car became inoperable again and needed another important part to keep it running, the same kind person helped her obtain the part, and her car remains operational to this day.

While it is easy to encounter Jesus in the Blessed Sacrament and in the Holy Scriptures, it is considerably more difficult to recognize and accept him disguised in the person of a transient individual such as Dorothy. Through the years, I have learned to care, accept and help these patients as they are, without passing judgment on them. As a physician, my job is to take care of the person in front of me to the best of my ability, regardless of all other considerations. It is not always easy, but neither is it impossible to listen to and embrace Dorothy's life as a reflection of Jesus—the one whom we believe, love, and serve. Thanks to God, Dorothy's condition has improved, she is smoking less, and is finding a purpose in her life through helping others as much as she can, within the circumstances and limitations of her own life.

Amidst a perpetual wave of technological advancements designed to bring increased convenience, safety, and opulence to our lives, it is all too easy to forget that times were not always so pleasant. Worse still, many of us fail to remember that, for some, the seemingly ancient threats of starvation, succumbing to the elements, and being utterly out of touch with the greater population are very real—and very current.

Let us remember that Jesus was born in a stable as a homeless baby. Soon after, he was on the run, looking for asylum in Egypt. Then, as he started his public ministry, he again became a homeless person. Jesus lived out in the open, sleeping harsh nights without the comfort of a pillow. In Matthew 8:20, he says, "Foxes have dens and birds of the skies have nests, but the Son of Man has nowhere to rest his head," referring to his own transient state. When he died in agony on the cross, he had no home and no possessions. Thus, Jesus himself was homeless for much of his life.

Jesus identifies with the poor, the needy, the hungry, the homeless, and the sick. He is very clear about this, as we read in Matthew 25:40 "...whatever you did for one of these least brothers of mine, you did for me." It is a mistake to make generalizations about the less fortunate. Each of these individuals has a unique story, and it does no good to blame the destitute for the terrible circumstances they face. We must instead recognize in them the face of Jesus, and challenge ourselves to take steps to help them as much as we can.

Generalized Anxiety

The dull glow of electric lights shone as candles on either side of a wooden box adorned with a crucifix. This, my earliest memory that I can recall to this day with startling clarity, was a mystery to me for four years of my life. What was this image, and how did it become so ingrained in my three-year-old mind that some 70 years later I can still recall it in such vivid detail? The answer would come when I was seven years old, when my father would unexpectedly reveal to me that Mama Celia, the only mother I had ever known, was not, in fact, my birth mother. Irma was my birth mother, he explained, and she had died when I was three-years-old. The box at which I had innocently stared as a toddler had been my biological mother's coffin. This was an earth-shattering revelation to me, and the resulting trauma would stay with me for several decades.

In my view, health is a three-pronged issue in which the physical, the mental, and the spiritual must all be properly managed. Merely having good physical health does not equate to living a happy and fulfilled life. Because mental illnesses commonly develop slowly over extended periods of time, the symptoms of such maladies often go overlooked until they are very serious and difficult to treat.

Anxiety is the most common mental illness, affecting more than 40 million adults in the United States. It is more prevalent in women than in men, with high rates in middle-aged and older adults, and relatively lower rates in adolescents. Generalized anxiety disorder is the most frequent anxiety disorder in primary care, being present in more than 22% of patients who complain of anxiety problems. It is therefore not surprising that many of my own patients have suffered from anxiety.

Once I have a long-standing patient-physician relationship with someone visiting my office, I am generally able to identify through non-verbal communication when something is amiss with one of my patients. I encourage them to explore their worries and fears with questions such as: "How things are going at home? With your spouse? With your children? Is there anything that bothers you? Are you happy with your life?" etc. Most patients will commonly share their feelings and emotions in response. I listen without passing judgment or dismissing their concerns, respecting their beliefs without imposing my own. My approach, however, is to treat the whole person, and balance the physical, emotional, and spiritual aspects of their lives. As such, I am less apt to suggest medications before exploring the role and positive impact religion and spirituality may have on his/her mental health.

Sandy was a 48-year-old single mother who lived with her two adult daughters in an apartment not far from my office. At age 44, she suffered a stroke with residual muscular weakness on the right side of her body, which rendered walking difficult for her. She did not have health insurance, and no further treatment or rehabilitation was taken. She also complained of a burning sensation with numbness and tingling especially in her right leg and foot.

Sandy was under unusual physical and emotional distress, and unable to obtain medical treatment. She stated that she had experienced excessive worrying and anxiety for a period of at least 6 months. She was also restless, unable to relax, and on edge at all times, and had chronic insomnia and panic attacks of almost daily presentation.

Fatigue, muscle tightness, palpitations, headaches, and difficulty were also among Sandy's symptoms. She became depressed at times, and though she desperately sought relief, she did not turn to alcohol or non-prescribed drugs. In view of all these factors, a diagnosis of generalized anxiety disorder was entertained.

I explained Sandy's medical conditions to her, and with her consent, we started her on the following treatment plan: 1) Remain on medications for neuropathy and secondary stroke prevention, 2) Take a short course of anxiolytic medication, with long-term use of an antidepressant; 3) Perform 30 minutes of daily exercise, as tolerated; and 4) Enhance relationship with Jesus by reading the Bible and praying daily for 15-20 minutes. Sandy was a non-practicing Catholic, and did not own a Bible, so I provided one for her, along with a helpful card that detailed the steps of mental prayer. Finally, I advised that she chronicle her thoughts and feelings in a daily journal.

Sandy could not afford psychological or cognitive behavioral therapy in conjunction with her medications. Because our primary focus was on improving Sandy's condition, her subsequent office visits were professional courtesies.

After two months, we began to witness remarkable improvements in Sandy's condition, as she diligently followed our recommendations. Indeed, it seemed a new, brighter chapter of her life started to be written, as she read the Bible, prayed, and attended Sunday mass regularly.

Another patient who comes to mind is *Mohan*. Mohan was a 58-year-old gentleman who emigrated from India. The owner of a small business, he was married, with two sons and one daughter. Four years before I met him, Mohan was hospitalized for a heart attack, and underwent angioplasty to keep one of his heart arteries open. He was very compliant with his cardiac diet and medications, and kept his regular appointments.

Toward the end of 2018, Mohan came to see me because of anxiety. He complained of persistent worrying, restlessness, neck stiffness, tensional headache, insomnia, and poor appetite. His constant worry caused him gastritis and recurrent chest pain (angina pectoris). He had also lost more than 10 pounds in the previous month. Mohan cried as he reported to me that he felt he had made a terrible mistake coming to the United States. He had left a well-established and profitable business in his homeland to come to this country at the request of his sister, who sponsored him. His sadness deepened as he explained that his 21-year-old daughter had attempted suicide after being bullied by her own friends, resulting in a weeklong hospital stay. Mohan reported that his son, too, had recently been rushed to the emergency department, and was in danger of harming himself or someone else. The grieving father went on to detail his son's addiction to pornography, inability to keep a steady job, and general lack of motivation. Finally, Mohan voiced his regrets that his children do not practice his Muslim faith. I moved my chair so that I could be close to Mohan, listened carefully as he shared his sorrows with me, and reassured him that I would do my best to help him. I even provided him with my personal cell number, so he could reach me at any time to talk. I also reassured him that I would continue helping his children, who were also my patients.

I explained Mohan's medical conditions to him, and what could be done about them. He consented to a short course of anxiolytic medication, as well as other medications to treat his gastritis, improve his appetite, and relieve his insomnia. I encouraged him to continue to perform his Muslim prayers five times each day, read the Quran, and write a journal. He declined to have cognitive behavioral therapy in conjunction with his medications, believing that he would be back to normal after a few weeks.

Mohan was worried that he was taking too much of my time, as I needed to see other patients waiting for me, but I reassured him that caring for him was important to me. "I will catch up with the other patients later," I explained.

Today, I am happy to report that Mohan's circumstances have greatly improved: the situation with his children has changed for the better, he has gained weight, and, after three months, he discontinued the anxiolytic medications.

The importance of a strong sense of religiosity and/or spirituality to an individual's mental wellbeing really cannot be overstated, as these imbue in a person a sense of purpose, a sense of connectedness, a desire for wholeness and harmony, a belief in a higher power, and a general sense of the value of life. For some, it can be all too easy to lose touch with these things, and in such cases even a person in excellent physical health may suffer debilitating consequences. Often it is not with medications but with a healthy dose of spirituality that the true cures to one's ailments are to be found.

"So do not worry about tomorrow, for tomorrow will bring worries of its own. Today's trouble is enough for today." — Mt. 6:34

Morbid Obesity

I am happy to say that I never experienced the aversion to waking up and going to school that some children feel. On the contrary, attending school was something I enjoyed; I was genuinely enthusiastic about learning, so the process never felt like a chore to me. My father, to whom handwriting was very important, made us practice "orthography" at home, so I was decently skilled in penmanship before I began the first grade. Early on, I developed what would become a lifelong love for the sciences, and looked forward to those classes in particular.

Well-organized extracurricular activities in the Peru of my childhood were sparse, as we lacked the clubs and student organizations that are so prevalent today. Sports—soccer in particular—and body building were popular after-school diversions among the boys, but my interests leaned more toward the academic than the physical, so I launched a sort of makeshift tutoring service. Chalk in hand and the pavement my endless blackboard, I would walk my fellow students through various subjects in the hours after school. As my classmates came to know more about math and science in these lessons, I came to know more about myself and my love of helping others.

The remainder of my free time outside of school was spent working with the local parish, serving in whatever capacity I could. I was a member of the Legion of Mary, a group of boys and girls who would meet once a month, pray the rosary, help the parish with catechesis, and visit the sick. This, too, helped me to recognize in myself an innate desire to help people in need, particularly the sick and the poor. Even as a young boy, I wondered who would care for the underprivileged, for the outcasts, for the weak.

The aforementioned love of science and interest in helping people would eventually drive me to become a doctor, where I have since had the great privilege of treating patients from all different backgrounds. Some patients present with conditions that are invisible to the eye, but are easily diagnosed and treated nonetheless. Of the illnesses that are outwardly apparent, perhaps the most prevalent—and among the most difficult to treat—is obesity, whose sufferers must deal with not only physical limitations of the disease, but also the anguish of being looked down upon by a misunderstanding public.

Obesity is a common, grave, and costly medical condition. More than two-thirds of United States adults and more than a third of the nation's children are overweight or obese. Over the last several decades, obesity rates have increased for all populations in the United States, and the country spends about $150 billion a year treating obesity.

The Body Mass Index (BMI) is a person's *weight* in kilograms divided by the square of his/her *height* in meters. In general, a normal BMI is 18.5 – 24.9, overweight is 25 – 29.9, and obesity is ≥ 30. Morbid obesity is a high-risk, Class 3 obesity, where the BMI ≥ 40. This chronic medical condition is associated with other health problems, including heart disease, stroke, diabetes mellitus, and certain types of cancer that are some of the leading causes of preventable and premature death.

Obesity (morbid, in particular) is a much more difficult condition to treat than almost anything else in primary care. Patients treated for this condition often reach a "plateau" and stop losing weight, in spite of adhering to well-designed weight loss programs, making behavior modifications (diet and exercise), and taking medications, if necessary. Patients who have reached this plateau not only find further weight loss extremely difficult to achieve but also have difficulty maintaining the progress they have managed to make.

I am reminded of *Bert*, a 40-year-old, native of Los Angeles, weighing more than 500 pounds, with a BMI of 73.83. He became obese as a teenager, and developed early hypertension, diabetes mellitus, gout, edema with cellulitis of the lower extremities, disc herniation of the lumbar spine, and bilateral knee arthritis. His difficulty walking and severe obesity gave rise to frequent infections of the skin folds in the lower abdomen and groin, resulting in swelling of the scrotum, and wound infections, which spread into his bloodstream (sepsis). This required a number of hospitalizations. Bert also had great difficulty taking showers and keeping his body clean and dry. In addition, his high blood pressure and diabetes mellitus (necessitating insulin injections) were challenging to control. To make matters worse, each of Bert's diseases frequently led to another associated condition. To counter pain, for example, he took over-the-counter anti-inflammatory medications on his own volition, which in turn provoked gastritis, water retention, increased blood pressure, and worsening of kidney function.

Bert's morbid obesity, slow walking, and shortness of breath on minimal exertion strongly limited his ability to hold a steady job, and made him generally undesirable to employers. He tried a variety of weight control programs to no avail, as he was not motivated enough to follow them diligently—he simply gave up. Bert was disabled and had basic health insurance that did not cover gastric surgery as a possible definitive therapy for his morbid obesity. He seemed to be living without living, going through the motions of life without looking forward to a brighter future, while sharing a home with his brother, who suffered from Down syndrome. For Bert, the depression associated with his obesity was just one more difficulty he was forced to embrace, and he was not willing to take medication to combat it.

My time with Bert was unique because of the unusual challenges he posed as the heaviest patient I had ever treated in my office. I took care as his physician to accept Bert as he was, and help him deal with the medical consequences that resulted from his weighing more than 500 lbs. I could not allow the extremity of the case to diminish in any way my dedication and full support for his well-being, despite the many ups and downs he experienced under my care. I knew that Bert had a deep-seated desire to lose weight and get better, but his lack of adherence to a low calorie American Diabetic Association diet made sustained weight loss nearly impossible. His self-control seemed to be losing a terribly difficult war, and his physical health was badly suffering as a result. It was a most disheartening situation for me to witness as his physician. Remarkably, though, not even in his darkest days did Bert feel sorry for himself or sulk about his predicament. For the four years he remained under my care before relocating to another county, Bert was always very friendly, and tried to maintain a positive outlook on his weight loss.

It seems somehow uncomfortable to recognize Jesus in the face and life of Bert, but with a clear spiritual disposition, it is possible to place the interests of this patient before any other personal motivation, and view him with the eyes of faith as a brother in Christ.

When contemplating morbid obesity, I also think of *Peter,* a 45-year-old who weighed more than 450 lbs., with a BMI of 52. Peter had a rare chronic vascular condition near his groin that caused clots in the arteries and veins of his left leg for which he underwent several procedures to remove these clots and keep his vessels unobstructed.

On two occasions, he had a pulmonary embolism, a life-threatening condition caused by a vein clot breaking off from his leg traveling to his lungs. This required him to take blood thinners, in addition to medications for hypertension, hardening of his heart arteries, heart failure and obstructive sleep apnea. The latter is a condition in which the throat muscles intermittently relax and block the airway during sleep. This repeatedly interrupted breathing rendered him fatigued, irritable, and sleepy during daytime, even though he was using a CPAP machine, which is designed to deliver mild air pressure to keep the airways open during sleep.

Peter came to my office with high expectations to improve his cardiovascular conditions, as I was recommended by one of his relatives. After a few months, I would become his primary care physician as well. Once his heart and vascular conditions were brought under control, we turned to the issue of his morbid obesity. Peter was subsequently enrolled in a number of weight management and exercise programs, but failed to maintain any steady weight loss. He would frequently note with frustration that he could not lose weight *"no matter what I do."* Sometimes he skipped meals for one day or more, but still could not lose a meaningful amount of weight. In spite of all his efforts, Peter's weight hovered around 450 pounds. Like Bert, Peter had limited health insurance that did not allow him access to more sophisticated treatments. He was forced to be placed on temporary disability.

Peter is a 6-foot-tall man with an obese body configuration and a pleasant demeanor. He remains my patient to this day, and, with the help of his wife, is able to keep his appointments and undergo all required testing. He is a Christian with a simple faith and an uneven prayer life. In our years together, I have come to know and appreciate

Peter, and have tried to help him to the best of my abilities. I am always humbled by his acknowledgement of such efforts, as we fight together on his most difficult weight loss journey.

I feel fortunate that I am able to report less precarious outcomes for some patients, some of whom were able to significantly improve their health. I think of *Jim*, who underwent gastric surgery at age 68. He used to weigh more than 390 pounds with a BMI of 50. For many years he suffered from hypertension, heart failure, diabetes mellitus, obstructive sleep apnea, hardening of the heart arteries with two previous angioplasties, and high serum lipids levels. For several years, he tried unsuccessfully to lose weight and keep it overtime. His morbid obesity resulted in knee joint degeneration, worsening sleep apnea, and diabetes out of control despite tolerable nonsurgical weight-loss treatments. Thus, since this is a clear indication for gastric surgery, he underwent a "gastric sleeve surgery" in which over half of his stomach was removed, leaving a thin vertical sleeve, in place of the normally sized stomach. Few months after, Jim weighed 236 pounds (BMI=29) which made him overweight but no longer obese. Subsequently, we discontinued his medications for hypertension, diabetes, and diastolic heart failure. Since then, he had a total left knee replacement and he continued losing weight steadily over the last 4 years.

I have known Jim and his wife for more than 25 years. He is a practicing Catholic and devoted family man, with an old-fashioned work ethic. Before gastric surgery, Jim was hospitalized multiple times because of comorbid conditions associated with his obesity. Jim is the kind of patient who always comes to see me without hesitation when he realizes something is wrong with his health. On one occasion, he had chest pain (angina pectoris), called my office, and went to the emergency room of the hospital where I was doing heart procedures.

This enabled him to receive an immediate heart angiogram, and took care of his heart condition right away.

Through my years treating Jim as a patient, we have experienced together both good and bad times, experiencing challenges in and out of the medical office. I have been a silent witness of the difficulties that Jim overcame on account of his robust fellowship with Jesus, as he prayed every day and accepted God's will in his daily life, while hoping for a better tomorrow. I noticed in him, for example, an unwaveringly optimistic attitude, even in the face of a total knee replacement surgery which led to infection and two subsequent surgeries. In spite of the high risk of complications associated with these surgeries, Jim's attitude remained positive, as he comfortably placed his total trust in Jesus.

For more than 25 years in my practice, we have provided a comprehensive program of medically supervised weight management to achieve and maintain a reduced weight over time. After an initial assessment that includes blood testing, the prescription provides behavior modifications to develop new healthy eating habits and break away from unhealthy patterns. Patients also receive nutrition counseling, aerobic exercise, nutraceuticals, medications, support group meetings, and follow-up consultations.

Esther is a 65-year-old lady with morbid obesity and history of high blood pressure, weighting 360 pounds with a BMI of 66. She has been in our program for about 3 years. She has lost 112 pounds, and her BMI now is 45. She is still morbidly obese, but she is doing much better, and has been taken off of medications for hypertension.

It is convenient to dismiss individuals suffering from severe obesity as responsible for the consequences of not attending to their diets in a disciplined manner, but this is neither constructive nor fair. My faith directs me against judging these patients and instead endowing them with the knowledge and tools to make the necessary—and very difficult—lifestyle changes toward becoming healthier and happier people. Encouragement and compassion are food for the soul, and it is from the determination to which these give rise that I believe truly effective diets begin.

Deafness

Most children look forward to their summer vacations. Whether they spend them off at camp, making new friends and seeing old ones, or remain indoors simply enjoying a respite from the monotony of school life, most young students count the days until that final bell rings and they are free for a few glorious months, until the next school year begins. I was not most children.

My summers were not spent in the company of friends or in the comfort of my bedroom pursuing hobbies. For me, the last day of school signified the beginning of another stint as a laborer in my father's candle factory. There I would spend my summers performing tasks that even many adults would find difficult, toiling for long hours in blistering heat. As a child I naturally lacked the strength to operate some of the machinery in the factory, so I would hang from levers and rely on the full weight of my body to get them to budge. This was exhausting work that would start early in the morning and carry on until 4pm, at which time I would often forgo the luxury of a bed and simply sleep on the floor.

I suppose, like other kids, I did count the days until summer, but not in joyful anticipation of what lay ahead. Mine was, perhaps, more an exercise in preparation for the hard work ahead of me. I despised this summer schedule of mine at the time, of course, but I had some sense that the labor would benefit me in the long run. And as this schedule carried on into my teen years, I began to understand that hard work and adversity build character—that resilience, perseverance, and a willingness to push through difficulties can give rise to powerful traits that last a lifetime.

Years later, I would see this phenomenon repeat itself in a number of my patients, to whose challenges my time in the candle factory would pale in comparison. These inspiring individuals would overcome physical limitations and demonstrate personal qualities that continue to impress me to this day.

I am reminded of 53-year-old *Linda*, who had been deaf since childhood. Linda had no children, but was married to a wonderful husband who would accompany her to her appointments and use sign language to help us to communicate with her. When I met Linda, she had multiple medical conditions and had recently undergone open-heart surgery to replace her aortic valve with critical stenosis. In spite of her serious medical conditions, which included diabetes, thyroid disease, heart failure, and degenerative disease of her cervical spine, she never expressed discontent about her illnesses or limitations. She was very compliant with her appointments, testing, and medications. I was always impressed by the cheerful way Linda conducted herself, despite her limitations. She was a woman of great spirit and courage, who lived a simple and happy life, taking one day at a time. She was patient and very well-mannered, and cared for her parents who lived close to her. At no point did I have to encourage Linda to accept her circumstances and find happiness; rather, I found myself learning from the example of an admirable woman who could smile when faced with tremendous adversity.

I think, too, of *Peter*, a 42-year-old man who developed partial deafness after multiple ear infections in his youth. As an adult, he continued to suffer from several allergies, recurrent respiratory tract infections, and hearing impairment, for which he wore hearing aids.

Recurrent sinus infections were so common for Peter that he learned to identify the onset of the symptoms, and would promptly schedule appointments with me to see me when they arose. My staff and I would communicate with Peter by using signs and speaking loudly. Despite his ailments, Peter steadily maintained a full-time job in a local office supply store. Like Linda, Peter found the strength to acknowledge and overcome his limitations without bitterness, instead approaching life with a beautiful optimism. It was my good fortune to care for him for two decades.

In observing how Linda and Peter adapted to their disabilities, I was reminded, in the first place, of how lucky I am to be able-bodied myself. More poignantly, though, I witnessed how the adversities they had faced had given rise to growth in other areas, such as amicability, friendliness, patience, and a greater sense of understanding and compassion for others. Personified in these extraordinary patients were so many of the lessons I had learned of adversity in my Christian education as a child. The trials Linda and Peter had faced in their lives had brought about fruitful self-reflection and an enlightened sense of life's true priorities. I was inspired to make a similar examination of my own life and evaluate how my own comparatively miniscule struggles have helped to shape me as a man. And while I can truly say that I would be happy to never see another candle factory, if those seemingly endless summers instilled in me but a fraction of the qualities I observed in Linda and Peter, I wouldn't change a thing.

Heart Transplants

Summer months in the Southern Hemisphere last from January through March, with school resuming on April 1st and lasting until December 20th, just before Christmas. I was always eager to return to school, not only to escape the candle factory, but to get back to learning, and my transition to high school was particularly exciting, as we began to tackle subjects in greater depth. The more intense curriculum brought with it a need for greater organization and better budgeting of one's time. I continued to tutor my classmates, now during school hours, after satisfying the minimum requirements for physical education and being set free. In truth, after about an hour of exercise, we were given the option to play either basketball or soccer—I chose math. There again putting chalk to pavement on the high school grounds, my classmates and I would go over problem after problem. I formulated a schedule that would allow me the time to attend all of my classes, complete all of my assignments, meet all of my deadlines, and continue to tutor anyone who asked for my help. Realizing that any one of those things could fall by the wayside if I failed to stick to this plan, I attended to it with absolute conviction. I would focus on academics from Monday to Friday, work at the candle factory on Saturday, attend mass Sunday morning, return to the candle factory to work for the rest of the morning, rest, and repeat. It was a busy and at times tiring schedule but it impressed upon me the importance of being well-organized and mapping out an agenda for oneself—traits that have proven invaluable to me in the years that have followed.

Nonetheless, I do on occasion find myself guilty of thinking that there are simply not enough hours in the day. Guilty, I say, in light of my having patients for whom this is literally the case—patients who are essentially living on borrowed time. Of these, perhaps none live with such difficulty as those awaiting heart transplants.

I am reminded of *Noah*, who was 8-years-old when he arrived from Mexico with his family in Los Angeles. The oldest sibling in a family of six, Noah took up work with a landscaping company after completing high school. Noah lived a relatively clean lifestyle, not drinking or using drugs, but he began to gain weight steadily, and developed diabetes mellitus (high blood glucose) in his thirties. He suffered a viral infection, causing a dilated and weak heart, and ultimately resulting in severe heart failure. By age 40, he was unable to work, because of shortness of breath on minimal exertion and episodes of near transient loss of consciousness. Since he was at high-risk for sudden cardiac death, in April of 2012, he had a cardioverter-defibrillator device (ICD) implanted, to stop his heart from beating dangerously quickly.

Noah was referred to me by his primary care physician in early February 2017. An ultrasound study of his heart revealed marked dilatation of the four chambers with a 23% function (normal = 50-80%) of the main pumping chamber of his heart. He had severe hardening of two of his three heart arteries; and underwent angioplasty (dilatation of the narrowed arteries) with the deployment of flexible tubes made of wire mesh (stents) that remained in place holding the arteries open. In addition, he had uncontrolled insulin-dependent diabetes mellitus and advanced chronic kidney disease, but he did not require dialysis. He was given optimal tolerable medical therapy, and referred to a ranked first heart transplant center.

By March of 2017, he was evaluated and placed on the heart transplant list. From then on, he was cared for by the heart transplant team and our office. Though Noah was receiving the finest medical care and was fully willing to comply with the prescribed instructions and medications, it was very difficult to keep Noah in adequate physical shape. Indeed, he was not able to tolerate, for example, a medication which would markedly improve his heart failure and prevent him from repeated hospitalizations; diuretics had to be cautiously used to balance his water retention with deteriorated kidney function and symptomatic drop of blood pressure. In addition, he received several shocks from his ICD, due to transient episodes of very dangerously fast heart beats.

Noah shared his frustrations with us, as he patiently waited for a heart transplant. I viewed Noah as an exceptional young man with multiple worsening medical conditions, powerless to work, unable to marry his fiancée of several years, and at times quite depressed. He was a practicing Christian Catholic who read and prayed the Bible regularly and had a close friendship with Jesus Christ.

Try to imagine what it must be like for a young man like Noah to wait for a life-saving heart transplant every day. Imagine living with constant fatigue, lack of energy, and shortness of breath while showering or getting dressed, for example, because end-stage heart disease has placed marked limitations on your daily activities. Imagine the uncertainty of being forced to live one laborious day at a time with a weak and enlarged heart, hoping and praying for the miracle of a heart donor before is too late. As I witnessed Noah's physical and emotional trials and tribulations, I encouraged him and prayed with him so that we both might see the half of the glass that is not empty.

Unfortunately, four weeks after Noah's last office visit with us, in October 2018, he complained of sudden onset of chills and fever in association with an infected wound in one of his thighs. The next day, he was rushed to a hospital and found to have "flesh-eating bacteria" disease. He received immediate intravenous antibiotics and urgent surgical removal of dead and infected tissue from the wound. The next day, as he was prepared to have a second operation, he expired, following several cardiac arrests. According to one of his sisters, it appeared as though he had had this localized skin infection for several days, but he had thought it would heal on its own, and therefore did not seek medical help.

Jon grew up in a Catholic family in the Midwest. Upon his honorable discharge from the Marine Corps at age 24, he met his future wife, Dinna, and got married a few months later. He then took a labor job, working rigorously in the railroad business, while Dinna tended to the household and cared for their three daughters. The family never missed Sunday mass at St. John Neumann Catholic Church.

At age 50, Jon had a dilated and weakened heart—cardiomyopathy—which resulted in heart failure, despite medical therapy. He was referred by his cardiologist to a medical center in Milwaukee, where he underwent a heart transplant in 1988 because of end-stage heart failure. Jon was 58 years old. Since then, Jon and his wife traveled 216 miles from his town in Michigan to Milwaukee, several times a year for further care for more than 28 years, without missing any scheduled appointments. Indeed, as expected, he developed several complications requiring hospitalizations and unscheduled appointments.

During all these years, following his transplant, Jon was able to enjoy the love and companionship of his wife, her family, and dedicated time to his hobbies including animal trapping, trout fishing, hunting, and gardening. His Catholic faith allowed him to overcome the ups and downs of his heart condition, as he joined his wife every night in prayer. "We attended mass every Sunday and I prayed every night for the miracle of Jon; for you, Doctor Joe; and everybody I knew," Dinna told me.

Later in life, unfortunately, Jon developed prostate cancer and underwent radiation treatment, from which complications arose. Around 2015, his local doctor suggested that Jon discontinue all his medications, including cyclosporine, an oral drug to prevent heart transplant rejection, but Jon refused. Finally, he was taken to the Veterans Administration Hospital, where another physician cared for him until his death in 2017, at age 81.

Jon had lived for 29 years with his cardiac transplant, and his wife was told that Jon "was the longest living patient with heart transplant" from this Milwaukee's medical center. (The world's longest-surviving heart transplant patient lived 33 years.) After I moved from Milwaukee, I had the good fortune of maintaining regular correspondence with Jon and his wife. For Dinna, Jon meant everything in her life. She remains heartbroken over her loss, treasuring the memories of a "wonderful, wonderful, wonderful man."

One line connected Noah and Jon, one link more profound than their ailing hearts: faith. I bore witness to the ways in which the faith of each of these patients carried them through the trials attendant to heart failure. I watched as faith gave them hope in their lowest moments, and was inspired by the resolve with which faith had endowed each man. In the end, the grace of God and the power of faith shielded men with deeply broken hearts from ever being deeply brokenhearted.

Alcoholism

As I sat back in preparation for this book and thought of the things I did for fun in my high school days, I got a shocking reminder of what a different era that was from today. In those pre-internet days, the most effective way to talk to a friend was to see him/her face-to-face, and if you wanted to watch a movie together, you would have to settle for whatever was playing at the cinema. Thousands of movies were not just a click away; rather one movie was several miles away. Those were simpler times, times before cell phones and constant stimulation, and drinking and drugs were seen as vices, not as diversions or rites of passage. Today, the frequency at which underage drinking takes place is startling, and the incidence of high school alcoholics is on a terrible upward trajectory.

In my own practice, I have dealt with a number of alcoholics, some of them very young. One such case that comes to mind is that of *Dahlia*.

Dahlia was born in 1987. She lived with her parents and her half-brother, Spencer. After two years, the family split, and Spencer went to live with his mother. This sudden fracturing of the family unit was difficult for Dahlia to process. She began to experience involuntary bed-wetting, and would wake up in the middle of the night crying.

In her teens, Dahlia was placed in a private, all-girls Catholic school, and despite her early difficulties, she went on to achieve excellence in both academics and sports. Dahlia developed into a beautiful, sweet, and charming girl who enjoyed dancing, modeling, and acting classes, and also served as a volunteer in her local Fire and Public Works Department. She graduated in June of 2005 with a 4.2 GPA, and was accepted into the University of California system.

In the summer following Dahlia's graduation, her family hosted Italian students for three weeks, and Dahlia was subsequently invited to visit Italy and stay with her former exchange classmates. Unfortunately, it was there that she began to drink alcohol and smoke. When Dahlia returned from her trip, she began skipping classes in her first semester at university to go to clubs to drink and party. By age 18, she had become an alcoholic, threated suicide, and required physical restraint after assaulting her mother. Despite this turmoil, she managed to graduate with honors from the University of California in just three years, and obtained her master's degree Cum Laude two years later.

By age 21, Dahlia was able to purchase alcohol, which resulted in her frequently driving under the influence, occasionally passing out in her truck (and other locations), and unable to answer her phone. This reached a peak when she was involved in a traffic collision and was arrested with a very high blood alcohol level. She was referred to several psychologists, specialists, and alcohol treatment centers, all of which failed to break her dependency on alcohol.

In 2013, Dahlia moved into her own apartment. Living on her own made it easier for her to drink more than 20 quart-size bottles of vodka per month, resulting in employers, neighbors, and friends calling her parents to report that they had not heard from her for days. This behavior led to the loss of four separate engineering positions and the subsequent loss of her apartment as well.

At that point, Dahlia's parents became desperate and brought her to my office in search of help. I asked her parents to leave the room so I could speak privately with Dahlia. We engaged in a long conversation in which she gave me an honest account of her troubles. This was followed by additional office visits, counseling, and medications to help her to stay sober and alleviate her withdrawal symptoms. She stopped drinking for a few months, and then began to miss her appointments, finally ending up in the intensive care unit (ICU) of the hospital with a variety of symptoms, including decreased awareness, confusion, eye muscle paralysis, dilated pupils, walking difficulty with loss of balance, rapid heartbeats, and epileptic seizures (Wernicke-Korsakoff syndrome). The neurologist who treated her stated that it was the worst case he had ever seen.

Eventually, Dahlia was released from the ICU, but she continued to drink. She entered a 100 day inpatient program in one Arizona's best treatment centers for alcoholism. Like the vast majority of addicted patients, she was also diagnosed with mood disorders. Upon completing the program, Dahlia was sent to a sober living home in California, from which she prematurely departed, and resumed her pattern of heavy drinking and unemployment.

In July of 2017, Dahlia severed ties with her boyfriend, after realizing he had been disloyal, and was in fact engaged to another woman. Remarkably, this was not to be the harbinger of her deeper decline into addiction, but the catalyst to her recovery. Fed up with the life she had been living, Dahlia gradually abandoned her drinking; moved in with supportive family friends, and regained employment with an aerospace company. These changes brought about happiness—and above all—sobriety in Dahlia's life. Since then, her lifestyle has greatly stabilized, though she has had occasional relapses, as expected.

My discussions with Dahlia revealed that her relationship with Jesus played a major role in her new attitude, as she tried to cope with herself, her purpose in life, her values, her feelings of inadequacy, her bitterness toward her parents, and the reality of her life today. I hope she will persevere in reading the Bible, prayer, writing her journal, and attending church services, all of which may contribute to her personal development and avoidance of a relapse to heavy drinking. I hope that the seeds planted in good faith will yield positive changing results in the life of Dahlia. Only prayer and time will tell if this success is to continue.

I encountered Jesus in Dahlia as a young needy person, who, like so many college students in the United States, fell victim to alcohol abuse. Dahlia's alcoholism gave rise to critical physical consequences that nearly ended her life. I knew from the beginning it would not be easy to help Dahlia to achieve a complete mental, physical, and emotional recovery from her addiction, but I was committed to assisting her in any way possible. Indeed, I always saw Dahlia and treated her as a baptized person, a sister in Jesus Christ, and not just another alcohol-addicted patient. I was presented with a unique opportunity to work in concert with Dahlia's parents and others, uniting in action, prayer, and a universal hope for a better Dahlia, our sister in the Lord.

Most doctors take some version of the Hippocratic Oath upon graduating from medical school, the focus of the oath being on the ethical treatment of patients and a doctor's duty to "do no harm." But long before I was ever a medical student, I made a vow to lead a Catholic life. Because I view myself as a Christian first and a doctor second, the focal point of my work is to help and care for the person in front of me, as I see him/her not merely as a patient, but as a fellow brother or sister. Sometimes providing this help means stepping beyond the world of cardiology and addressing problems of an entirely different sort. When I am able, I do this to the best of my ability, in any capacity. That, for a Catholic and a physician, is at once my duty and my joy.

Loneliness

"Why would you want to be a *matasano* (quack)?"—
that was the response I received when, at the age of 19, I announced
to my father that I had chosen to study medicine. "Medicine is for
people who have money to study," he continued. "We're middle class.
But I'll tell you what: From now on, you can continue to have your
room and meals in this house, but the rest—tuition, books, and other
expenses—you have to take care of yourself." I had made up my
mind that I would go to medical school, so I agreed to the deal right
away; the money I would have to figure out later. I applied to the only
local school of medicine, at the National University in my hometown, and after a total of eight written exams taken every other day,
I was awarded a spot to begin my undergraduate studies.

Part-time work did not exist in Peru at the time, so I would need
to devise a different plan to support myself. It seemed to me that the
most logical choice was tutoring. I had long ago discovered a joy for
teaching, and if those afternoons drawing math problems on the school
pavement were to be counted, you could say I had over a decade of
work experience under my belt. But this time I would have to charge
for my services. I spread word of my availability locally, and began
spending my weekends tutoring wealthy students in math, chemistry,
and physics. This endeavor went well enough that I was indeed able to
cover my expenses.

A short time later, I made the decision to leave home altogether,
becoming a teacher at the Minor Seminary of the Archdiocese of

Trujillo, outside of the city, and living on the premises for several months. I made this decision following a disagreement with my father, who scaldingly opined that I would likely divert all my attention to my girlfriend at the time and forget about becoming a doctor entirely.

Despite living in a comfortable room in the seminary, leaving home by my own volition was an unplanned experience, and I soon felt lonely and desolate in my new surroundings. That said, the experience matured me, and just before I started my graduate studies in medicine, I returned home and developed a close friendship with my father. It seems that my time away was good for both of us.

But as I have found all too frequently in my practice, absence does not always make the heart grow fonder.

Gail was born into a family of eight siblings—seven girls and a boy. She remained single throughout her life, living with her parents and working quite contentedly as a lawyer, until the death of her father, some 14 years ago. Gail was not prepared for this event. She was very close to her father, and would have long conversations and pray with him on a daily basis.

Though she continued to live with her mother, Gail began to feel desolate, empty, and unwanted. She saw to all her mother's needs, but felt that she was not as loved by her mother as her other sisters were, as her mother seemed to prefer spending time with Gail's sisters.

Then, in 2016, Gail experienced another shock when her mother passed away. Now she was forced to live by herself in an empty home with no one to communicate with. Disputes formed within the family, and Gail and her siblings were no longer on speaking terms. At the age of 66, Gail became worried about what would happen to her as she grew older. "*I may get sick. I'm afraid of dying. And what will happen when I die? Who will bury me?*" she asked herself. Her feelings of sadness and emptiness intensified. There were mornings when she did not want to rise out of bed, but she forced herself to go to work to make a living and survive. Gail was devoid of all goals or events to look forward to.

Under these very difficult circumstances, Gail says that it is her faith in Jesus, her Savior and Merciful Master, that keeps her alive and going. She thinks often and prays to God to face and overcome her loneliness. "I pray and meditate on the gospels, pray the rosary and other devotions every day," she reported to me. "That helps me get through the day, especially in these months of the COVID-19 pandemic, when I'm forced to stay home alone." Gail cries easily, but does not want to take medications, and cannot afford a counselor or psychologist. She cooks, cleans the house, reads books, takes care of herself, and gets her necessities by way of a neighbor. With Jesus at the center of her life, Gail is more at peace now, and her faith in him has become stronger.

Another patient who comes to mind is *Rosie*, who arrived in Los Angeles in 1963 as a 27-year-old certified public accountant. She met her future husband in a local parish and got married one year later. The couple had two sons. As their boys grew up, Rosie continued to work as an accountant, and her husband worked as an engineer for an aerospace company.

In later years, Rosie and her husband would see their sons marry and produce two wonderful grandchildren. The couple carried on living a comfortable life and enjoying their retirement, until 2012, when Rosie's husband, my patient of 19 years, developed severe heart failure and passed away. Since then, Rosie has lived by herself at home.

As one would expect, it was very difficult for Rosie to adjust to life without her husband. Her sons and grandchildren would visit on occasion, providing temporary relief to her sadness, until at last she grew accustomed to living by herself. Though she had come to terms with her circumstances, Rosie remained a lonely person, communicating with family and friends solely by phone and the internet. She continued to have a clear mind and remained very good with numbers, keeping her family's financial affairs under control. At 78, she was relatively healthy, apart from having rheumatoid arthritis and high cholesterol. Then, in 2014, she was again devastated by the death of her youngest son.

Rosie describes herself as a person of great faith in God. "I accept everything that God sends me every day with love, without complaining about it," she says. "Maybe God thinks I am a superwoman, because He sends me more troubles than I can handle. God knows what He is doing, but I don't. He must have a reason for me to suffer with these illnesses and other difficulties." Indeed, Rosie developed a difficult-to-treat neuropathy in both legs, resulting in constant and severe discomfort.

Rosie's faith in Jesus started when she was a teenager. After graduating as an accountant, she attended a religious order in her native South American country. She abandoned this pursuit after a few months, but her faith has continued to develop ever since. Now, at 84, she still recalls some of the difficult moments and the disappointments she suffered through, but feels no resentment for her circumstances, as she lives by her father's advice: *Do not feel hate, because hate is like poison that will eventually corrode the container of your body, and will eat you up.* "Whatever has happened in my life, Jesus gave me as a gift," she states. "I don't keep bad feelings or hold any grudges toward anyone."

Rosie says that she is looking forward to doing the will of God, adding, "I don't know why he is keeping me alive." Rosie has no fear of death; rather, she is ready to die anytime and be in the presence of God. "My faith and love for God is unconditional," she says. "I know He will never leave me alone, and He will always be by my side. When I am in a bad situation, I say, 'Please, Jesus, help me,' and he does."

Rosie claims that she has experienced real miracles of God in her life. She reports an event some three years ago, in which she wandered into the kitchen of her home for a late-night snack, after having trouble sleeping. Suddenly, a strong bright light flashed over the room, and Rosie almost passed out. She found herself lying on the floor, shouting "Jesus, Son of God, please help me!" From that moment forward, she has not used any inhalers for her life-long chronic bronchial condition, as it seems to have resolved to the point of requiring no medications.

Like many of my patients, Rosie does not attend mass regularly, nor does she have a set of devotional practices in her daily routine. Nonetheless, she assures me she knows Jesus and has a friendly relationship with Him as the main focus of her life and ready to withstand anything.

A solitary life, though not happy, does allow for much self-reflection. In the cases of both Gail and Rosie, spending extended periods of time alone with their own thoughts seems to have stirred in them a desire to tie up loose ends with friends, family, and God. The two women share a desire to be in good graces with the ones most important to them before the end comes. This is certainly a worthy conviction, but why should one delay such reparations until the final moments? It is well to trust in God and the promise of heaven to guide us in the afterlife, but so long as we live, we must also identify and keep close the ones who matter to us most. And if, by chance, we should outlive our earthly companions, let us remember, like Gail and Rosie, that we are never truly alone.

"...I am with you always, even to the end of the age"
— *Matthew 28:20*

Hypertension

My first two years of medical school were spent in classrooms learning basic sciences, including anatomy, physiology, microbiology, and pharmacology. Then, for the next three years, the learning took place in hospitals, where my classmates and I rotated through different services, including general medicine, laboratory medicine, surgery, pediatrics, and OBGYN. This system allowed us the opportunity to see patients with a wide range of complaints, and to learn from our superiors how to approach treating them.

In those days (the early 1970s), routine medical checkups were all but unheard of, as the costs associated with visiting a medical center were prohibitively high to the average person. It was common for people with minor to moderate ailments to visit pharmacies instead of doctors' offices, relying on the advice of apothecaries and their over-the-counter remedies. In general, the average person would only come to the hospital if all other options had been exhausted, and as a result, we tended to see patients whose illnesses were more serious in nature. A common condition among these patients was hypertension (high blood pressure), which left a strong impression on me for not only its high rate of occurrence, but also its devastating effects that came seemingly out of nowhere. Patients who appeared fine at the end of my shift one day could be gone or paralyzed the next, following a stroke. Perhaps most troubling of all was the fact that these outcomes could have been prevented with earlier detection and treatment.

By witnessing these events firsthand as a student, I came to understand early on that high blood pressure is a silent killer. Many of our patients with malignant hypertension were in terrible danger and did not even know it, as their symptoms ranged from minor (headaches, dizziness) to non-existent. It was both saddening and frustrating to see the lives of these men and women in their 40s and 50s claimed by cerebrovascular accidents resulting from a serious medical condition they did not know they had.

I am happy to say that medical checkups are much more common these days, and we have better treatments as well. As a result, hypertension is both easier to detect and easier to treat. Nonetheless, it remains a common ailment and one I continue to treat with vigilance on a daily basis.

I think now of *Nolan*, a 37-year-old male from Central America, with a long history of arterial hypertension. Nolan was a young and ambitious person with good manners, who was determined to become the best version of himself. Initially, he worked for a freight company as a truck driver. Later, he purchased his own truck and became independent, before starting his own company. He married a young lady, and purchased a new home. The couple had their first daughter together, with a second following four years later. Things seemed to be going very well indeed for Nolan.

Unfortunately, he was not so well-situated medically. Despite my constant and repeated advice to take his blood pressure medications every day, Nolan often failed to do so. He would visit my office with the "slight headache" associated with very high BP readings, because he did not take his medications, he ran out of his medications, or misplaced the prescription. We would then bring his BP under control in the office, and issue more samples and prescriptions to Nolan on a monthly or bimonthly basis. Multiple times, with the help of an audiovisual aid on the wall, I attempted to impress upon him about the need to keep his hypertension under control—regardless of whether he noticed any symptoms—to avoid potential deadly complications. I would explain clearly that arterial hypertension is one of the well-known "silent killers," along with high blood glucose (diabetes) and high cholesterol.

After several years under my care, Nolan experienced the loss of his mother, leaving him depressed for some time. I discussed with him my own experience losing my mother when I was three years old, and encouraged him to develop a more personal relationship with Jesus through daily prayer and reading the New Testament.

In 2005, following the advice of an older brother he deeply respected, Nolan discontinued his blood pressure medications, and began consuming raw garlic instead. Around Christmas that year, he left on a vacation to Guatemala with his wife and two daughters. As soon as their plane landed at the airport, Nolan complained of a severe headache to his wife. When the paramedics arrived, his systolic BP was above 240 mmHg (normal is below 130 mmHg). He suffered intracerebral bleeding and died in the hospital a short time later.

In early January of 2006, Nolan's wife called to apprise me of the circumstances of his death. I asked her to come to my office with her daughters. I cried when I saw and embraced his wife, her four-year-old daughter, and the baby of about six months of age in her arms. From a physician's standpoint, it was a particularly heartbreaking moment as Nolan's death could have been avoided, if only he had taken his prescribed medications.

It is unfortunate that Nolan did not fully believe that hypertension is a silent killer. He was usually asymptomatic, only experiencing headache and dizziness when his BP was critically high. I regret that in spite of my warnings, Nolan seemed confident that he would live for a very long time, and never became fully convinced of the need to take his medications as directed.

This tragedy illustrates the importance of listening to and following the medical advice and recommendations of your health care provider. The friendly advice given by well-intentioned family and friends may not necessarily apply to your specific health condition, and must never supersede the recommendations of a trained physician.

Next, I think of *Edward,* a 48-year-old known to have hypertension. His grandfather, father, a paternal uncle, and one of his brothers died at a young age because of complications of hypertension and heart disease. Edward complained of morning headache and lightheadedness for several months. He was aware of his high blood pressure, and had been taking medications to control it, until he lost his health insurance. He was subsequently referred to us by a close friend.

When I first saw Edward, his blood pressure was dangerously high. He was treated with four medications, in combination, and his hypertension was finally controlled in a few weeks. Further testing showed increased thickening of the heart walls, hardening of his heart arteries, renal failure and higher-than-normal levels of lipids in his blood. He was treated accordingly, for each of the above medical conditions, and he is doing much better.

A few years ago, *Edward,* a computer engineer, was ready to retire at the prime of his life. Unfortunately, the investments he made turned out south and overnight he lost several millions of dollars and ended up living in his car with his wife and children. They were helped by a local organization focusing on the homeless. Gradually, he was able to overcome his poverty; and, as soon as he could, he materialized a promise that Edward and his wife made: to create and run a foundation to help the homeless. He confided to me that it was amazing to see that the more he was giving the little he had, the more he was receiving with referrals and job opportunities which allowed him to take care of his family and the foundation beyond his expectations.

It was not difficult to recognize Jesus in the face and life of Edward. As a Christian, he is an instrument of the Lord. Having experienced in his own life what it means to live marginalized without a home, he is now able to share what he has with others who are homeless, and help them to live with dignity.

When I reflect on my encounters with Nolan, Edward, and the countless other patients with hypertension I have treated throughout my career, I cannot detach myself from the notion that, in the modern era, this so-called "silent killer" need not, in fact, be silent or deadly. We are told in Proverbs 3:5 to "Trust in the Lord with all your heart, and do not rely on your own insight." This humbling advice does not suggest that we are intended to be naive and senseless, but instead reminds us that we cannot know everything. God endows each of us unique gifts, which, in the best of cases, we are able to cultivate to a point of expertise, and use our skills to enrich the lives of others. We must trust God always, but so, too, must we not be too proud to trust the advice of learned men and women who would help us.

Difficult Patients

Gratitude was in no short supply among the patients I saw in my early days as a medical student and intern in Peru. Though, as I mentioned before, the cost of visiting a medical center in those days often discouraged people from coming for problems they felt were less-than-critical, once such patients did arrive, they were always trustful of the medical staff and very grateful for the help we gave them.

Ignorance, on the other hand, was plentiful, for also embedded in the way of life was a culture of traditional medicine, old wives tales, and a general misunderstanding of medicine. It was not uncommon to encounter patients whose conditions had been worsened by herbal remedies recommended to them by friends or family members. Imagine my dismay when I learned from a young mother that she had taken the advice of a neighbor and served a tea made from animal droppings to her son to calm his upset stomach. While to you, the reader, the notion of drinking any sort of guano is more likely to cause than to cure an upset stomach, this mother, who only wanted the best for her son, simply did not know better. There was also a peculiar view among the general public that doctors with higher fees were necessarily better doctors. And the modern fixation on the evils of vaccines is really not so modern, as many people feared and refused them in Peru in the 1970s, believing unfounded word-of-mouth stories about illnesses resulting from vaccinations. At times, we had to put a great deal of effort into re-educating patients who had fallen victim to folktales and superstition.

Today, the climate is very different. Rather than knowing too little, patients in this internet-enabled age sometimes believe they know it all, and we find ourselves in the difficult position of having to convince them of what is actually the case. At times, patients are outright rude. Some have arrogant and demanding attitudes, and voice grievances about the smallest of details, from the way in which they were greeted by the receptionist to the temperature of the exam rooms. Others do not seem to have any interest in listening to the very medical advice one would assume they came in to receive.

In short, some patients really require patience.

"Sir, do you speak English?" a female physician asked *Feliciano*, as she entered the examining room. Feliciano was an 88-year-old retired lawyer with rapid irregular heartbeats and heart failure. Judging by his name, the doctor thought he might speak only Spanish, in which case she would need to call a Spanish speaking doctor to see him in her place. The question infuriated Feliciano, who spoke English, and he became verbally hostile toward the doctor, forcing me to intervene, apologize, explain to him why he had been asked the question, and carry out the rest of his office visit in an amicable manner.

Unfortunately, this was not the first time that Feliciano displayed such a difficult attitude. He was inconsistent in attending his appointments, arriving at the office whenever he pleased, and objecting to having to wait to be seen. He questioned the necessity of tests that were ordered for him and the dosage and frequency of his prescribed medications. Even the temperature of the exam rooms was objectionable to him. I would frequently find myself explaining to Feliciano that we were doing our best to serve and care for him. On each of his visits, I would listen to his complaints, keep my composure, write his medications in a medications table list, and send him on his way. Of course, there were moments I became impatient and frustrated with Feliciano, but I reminded myself that his behavior could have been due to his cognitive impairment.

I am reminded also of 77-year-old *Nelly*, my patient of 27 years, who would come to my office in the company of her husband. Nelly had high blood pressure, heart disease, joint pain, and mild Parkinson's disease. On several occasions, she spent the office encounter telling me the minor unusual grievances she has experienced since her last office visit, for which she demanded to see various specialists. "Why do I have more moles on my right forearm than on my left?" she would ask, for example. "Why does my left hand feel colder than the right, but only in the morning, and not all the time?" For some such inquiries there were easy explanations, but for others, I would have to tell her I simply didn't know.

Nelly would also call the office demanding to talk to me, insisting that she had important questions that could not wait. I would return these calls between patients or at the end of the day. She would also place calls to make premature inquiries about the results of tests that had only just been performed. Regardless of how tired and/or hungry I may be at the end of a long work day, I have a policy to return all phone calls before leaving the office. I would always do my best to handle Nelly's concerns with a supportive attitude. I make it a point to remember that, although a patient like Nelly's concerns may be trivial from a medical standpoint, they can be of the utmost importance to the patient, and I must treat the matters accordingly.

Henry similarly comes to mind. Henry's blood pressure was dangerously high, at 190/113 mmHg (normal < 130/80) when he came to see me in July 2017. The 71-year-old practicing Christian senior had hypertension and heart disease, with a previous stent in one coronary artery. Henry also had very high cholesterol levels. His conditions had been followed for years, and he had taken his heart medications as prescribed, so why was his blood pressure suddenly so high?

I would soon learn that Henry had begun reading a book written by a naturalist doctor, and following the book's recommendation, had begun taking "natural herbs' to control his blood pressure and heart disease. "Dr. Caceres," he said, "I am no longer taking any of the four medications you prescribed. I know what I'm doing. My knees don't hurt anymore either. I urge you to read this book. I'm still going to church daily, but I refuse to take any medication anymore." I explained in detail the risks involved with hypertension left out of control, adding that we do not know the real cause of the disease in more than 90% of patients. I warned him that the complications include stroke and heart attacks, and reminded him of my long experience in the field. Nonetheless, he continued to refuse to take any medication for his high blood pressure and other conditions, allowing me to document this in his electronic records and exonerating me from any responsibility for his decision. A few months later, Henry stopped coming for his office visits. We made several attempts to contact him by phone, but his number was no longer in service.

In dealing with patients with heart disease, especially those with diabetes mellitus, it is important to keep in mind that the presence or absence of symptoms do not correlate with the severity of their heart condition. Such was the case with *Franco*, a 77-year-old with diabetes mellitus, four coronary artery bypass grafting surgery, chronic systolic heart failure, a permanent pacemaker, and recurrent chest pain (angina pectoris). After erroneously concluding that his blood sugar had gone up as a side effect of his heart medication, Franco discontinued the medication without consulting me. As a result, his heart condition worsened to the point that he required hospitalization.

One of the problems we encounter with some patients is the fact that, despite our verbal and written warnings (in English and Spanish as required), they are noncompliant in taking the medications, or reduce or stop some medications altogether, blaming them for new— often very mild—symptoms that appear. They will do this even with medications they have been taking for extended periods without issue. In other instances, a medication prescribed will be changed by the pharmacist because of insurance coverage, or the patient will take the medication on a different schedule than originally prescribed. Another difficulty emerges when patients expect doctors to identify the names of their medications based solely on descriptions of the colors and shapes of pills they are taking, e.g., "the round blue one."

It is part of being a physician to encounter difficult patients who, in spite of doing one's best to serve them, cannot seem to be pleased. Equally trying are patients who recognize the seriousness of their medical conditions, but will not take their prescribed medications. These situations bring annoyance and frustration to the diligent practitioner, particularly if they come in the middle of a very busy day, as maintaining one's self-control and resolving the issues in a professional manner requires an extra dose of stamina. Under these circumstances, I usually take a deep breath, say a short mental prayer, and do my best for the person I have in front of me. This can be truly exhausting, leaving me quite spent at the end of a long day in which I have tried to do what was best for the patient and not necessarily what was best for me. The difference between ending such a day on a high note or a low one can be as simple as remembering the following:

A soft answer turns away wrath, but a harsh word stirs up anger. — Proverbs 15:1

Charity

In Peru, the government requires one year of civil service as a sort of reimbursement from students who received no-cost medical education at National Universities. The location of this duty is determined randomly by a sort of lottery, and most doctors hope to be placed in one of the big cities. I did not receive such a placement. When I graduated medical school in 1977, I was assigned to a medical center in the district of Moro, some 120 miles south of Trujillo. Here, in this largely agrarian society, I spent my earliest year as a doctor, working in service to the local community.

I was the first doctor ever to be assigned to Moro, and as such, I saw a wide variety of patients, sometimes under extraordinary conditions. Working in a rural environment meant encountering patients with conditions unique to agricultural workers. For example, I dealt with cases of herbicides poisoning, resulting from farmers coming in contact with the toxic pesticide parathion while spraying down vineyards.

House calls were quite common. On one occasion I was summoned in the middle of the night to the home of a young woman in labor. I arrived to a dark room with the expectant mother lying on blankets on the floor. The delivery was complex, as the umbilical cord had become wrapped around the baby's neck, but with the help of a flashlight and some improvisation—I used my finger to dislodge the cord—both the baby and the mother were fine. What a far cry this was from the calm and sterile environment of the hospital where I had finished my training, but it afforded me the opportunity to help someone in need, and that is all that mattered to me.

This was not to be the last—or even the most remarkable—time I would assist with the birth of a child in Moro. In fact, one such event, only four months into my time in Moro, would change my life forever.

I vividly recall her arrival. A young woman of the fields, she was not well-educated and did not seem terribly concerned with the fact that she was in labor. Astoundingly, this indifference carried on even after the baby had been delivered. The young lady showed hardly any interest in holding her newborn daughter; indeed, she wanted nothing to do with the child at all. I was not equipped to deal with such a situation, and frankly neither was the district of Moro—there was no child services bureau or similar agency one could call. I did as I suppose one does when one has no answers—I called my parents.

What followed was a whirlwind of events that took place with a swiftness that amazes me to this day. Within hours of delivering the baby, I was in a cab from Moro to Trujillo in the company of a nurse and the newborn. One stop at the mayor's office, and the baby was off to meet her new parents—my parents. That's right—they had agreed to adopt her when I called them, and the baby I was to deliver to them was my sister Beatriz.

Even absent this momentous event, I would still mark my time in Moro as formative for me as a physician, as I used the opportunity to become better acquainted with the profession and more familiar with the local people. In the process, I came to know more about myself, as well. And though the job was not rewarding from a financial standpoint, it was in other ways a dream come true, for I had done it: I had become a doctor and I was truly helping those in need.

As I write this now nearly half a century later, I thank God that the same desire to act in service to those in need remains intact in me. I have always endeavored to channel any success my practice is given into pathways to better care for my patients. This means keeping the office equipped with state-of-the-art systems and devices, and creating the warmest and most welcoming environment for them. And in 2017, my wife and I were very proud to establish "The Jose & Fe Caceres Foundation."

The Foundation was established to provide aid to new cardiac patients who must undergo comprehensive cardiovascular evaluations. These assessments include physical examinations, blood tests, chest X-rays, electrocardiograms, and ultrasound studies of the heart at rest and at the peak of exercise (stress echocardiogram), and are used as a way to document the presence or absence of significant hardening of the coronary arteries that supply blood and nutrients to the heart muscle. The Foundation paid for 75% of the total charges for these services. In order to qualify for this support, a new patient simply signs an affidavit that affirms his/her lack of healthcare insurance and inability to pay for the services, based on low annual income.

Since 1993, we have aided patients who were referred to us by their pastors or religious leaders, regardless of their ethnic backgrounds, languages, religions, sexual orientations, or ability to pay for our services. The Foundation was established as a way to provide medical services for patients who do not qualify for medical assistance from the State, as well as a substantial number of undocumented people who cannot afford the services out-of-pocket. We have proudly been able to help a sizable number of patients with confirmed or suspected heart conditions referred from different non-profit clinics.

One such patient was *Hilda*, an elderly woman in urgent need of a permanent pacemaker to control her abnormal slow heart beats, which were causing her to faint. The implantation of a pacemaker was possible because of the Foundation as well as the low-cost of the device provided by the manufacturer.

Another patient was *Ray*, a 59-year-old man, with heart disease, symptoms of acute heart failure, no income, no federal benefits, no unemployment--no means to pay. He arrived at the office not knowing about the foundation, and worried about how he would pay for the services he very much needed. We told him about the Foundation, he wrote a declaration, a simple application was processed, and 75% of complete evaluation services were covered by the Foundation.

From a financial standpoint, the Foundation was naturally not gainful. What is more, it soon came to our attention that some people had begun abusing the Foundation's aid, and the amount of recipients rose sharply. We were forced to change our strategy, closing the Foundation in 2019, and instead offering a low-cost package for the same services. The price point for this bundle has been set at a cost affordable to nearly everyone.

Many Foundation patients have continued to come to the office for continuity of care during the last several years. It is not uncommon to encounter asymptomatic patients with malignant hypertension, fast irregular heartbeats, or out-of-control diabetes that place them at high risk for a disastrous acute event. Such patients can be easily managed if they are aware of their medical conditions, and we are proud to offer services to them that fit within their budgets.

While not every Christian is a priest or pastor, every Christian is a minister; that is, all Christians must use their gifts and talents in service to others. It is a joy to work in service to my patients today, the same as it was at the start of my career. In this way, I am working, too, in service to the Lord, and there is no simply higher purpose.

> *"...give, and it will be given to you. A good measure, pressed down, shaken together, running over, will be put into your lap; for the measure you give will be the measure you get back."*
> — *Luke 6:38*

Alzheimer's Disease

In 1978, all of my siblings in Peru—including now one-year-old Beatriz—congregated at the local parish of the Miraculous Medal to celebrate the 50th anniversary of Antonio and Celia, our parents. Now in their 70s, they had seen all but their two youngest children grow up to become busy professionals who were not often afforded the time to return home for visits. Our reunion made the event all the more special, as we used the occasion to catch up with one another, share memories, and express our gratitude to God Almighty for keeping our parents in relatively good health.

As a proud expression of our Catholic faith lays the foundation of our family life, it was important to us that we celebrate not only the 50 years of marriage, but also God Himself, as it was only possible through His good grace. At 6 pm, we began with a Mass of Thanksgiving in which I walked my mother down the center aisle of the church, and my eldest sister Bita accompanied my father. There we prayed and thanked God for all the wonderful blessings he had given us as a family that still continued to grow and prosper. Afterwards, friends and neighbors joined us at our home for dinner and dancing. We were a middle-class family, so it was a modest affair, but the chance to be together again for this *bodas de oro* was indeed more valuable than gold itself.

Some forty years later, I can still remember the event as if it were yesterday, for its beauty and its significance to my family. In the course of a single day, we created the sort of memories that can last a lifetime.

How thankful I am, not only to have taken part in such a joyous celebration, but also to have the faculties to recall it with such clarity. Not all people are so fortunate.

Imagine finding yourself holding this book right now, but not knowing at all what it was about, or indeed why you were holding it to begin with. You determine that you must have picked it up to do some light reading, and though you see you are in the middle of the book, you flip back to the beginning, as you can't recall the previous chapters. Now imagine that this scenario repeats itself when you are halfway through Chapter Two. Then again when you reach Chapter Four. This is but one of the many frightening events that might face a patient suffering from the progressive cognitive, behavioral, and functional neurological disorder known as Alzheimer's disease (AD).

Over the years, I have seen a growing number of patients with Alzheimer's disease. While measures such as the Mini-Mental Status Exam (MMSE) and deeper neurological tests provide an effective means of diagnosing the condition, there remains at present no treatment that can stop the progress of the disease. This means that all AD patients will inevitably reach a point at which they can no longer live safely in their own homes, and must subsequently be placed in skilled nursing facilities where adequate management and supervision can be provided. It has been truly challenging for me to witness this deterioration first-hand over the years, and I regret that I could write volumes on the heartbreaking experiences I have had with some 20 different individuals who have succumbed to this terrible debilitation. For the purposes of this work, however, I shall focus on one particularly poignant case that highlights not merely a man in decline, but the truth of human dignity and the presence of Christ within him.

Felix was born in 1930 in the Philippines. He worked for an electric company in Manila for many years, until his retirement in 1993. He was married to *Bebet* for 65 years, and the couple had four daughters and one son. The family was very involved in the local parish activities: they attended mass faithfully, and every year they prayed the rosary for a week as the statue of the Virgin Mary was customarily brought to their home. Bebet was in fact in charge of instituting this practice in every local home throughout the year. Food in Felix and Bebet's household was equally distributed, and each family member did his or her share of duties to keep the household running smoothly. Like most middle-class families in the Manila area, they lived a relatively happy life.

Felix and Bebet emigrated to the United States and became my patients in 1995. Later, his children, too, would be in my care. Felix underwent replacement of his aortic valve and had irregular heartbeats, in addition to other medical conditions that required blood thinners. His wife, too, dealt with medical problems, and succumbed to breast cancer in 2009, at the age of 79.

In early 2015, Felix began repeating the same questions over and over again to his daughters, and frequently became disoriented and confused. His daughter related to me an event during which Felix asked to be taken to the bank, and remarked upon arriving there that he was not in the right place. After being taken to a different bank branch, he stated, "This is not the place where I catch fish. Please check if there is a fish in that pond where I left my bait." Another time, while in his bedroom, he screamed, "There are spiders crawling up and down the wall! Don't step there! There are ants all over the floor!" There were instances of him clapping his hands to "kill mosquitos" that were not in fact there. On another particularly frightening occasion, he was found roaming the streets "looking for the bathroom."

Felix was diagnosed with Alzheimer's dementia, and began taking two different medications, without significant improvement. His children, who lived with him, quickly learned to separate the behavioral effects of the disease from their beloved father's actual intentions. They made the decision to become his caregivers and keep him at home for the rest of his life, taking turns administering to him. Though Felix would lose track of recent events, become lost in his own home, and even forget the names of his children, he maintained a healthy appetite and good speech. He was still able to come to visit my office in a wheelchair, and complained of intermittent tremors of the hands and legs. I vividly recall an instance in which he told his children: "Dr. Caceres is going to cut my hair. I am his gardener."

By September 2019, his dementia worsened, requiring extensive care. He began to experience urinary incontinence, and stopped communicating verbally, relying instead on facial expressions and hand gestures. This was followed soon after with difficulty chewing and eating, necessitating a pureed diet. At last, he became bedridden, and required caregivers to physically rotate him in his bed, to avoid pressure ulcers. One of his daughters slept dutifully in a bed near Felix's own bed, and listened as he moaned day and night. A home health nurse came to see him several times a week, updating me on Felix's condition, and I went personally to check on him over the Christmas season. He recognized me at once and smiled, which warmed my heart.

When I left, Felix lay on his bed with his eyes open, enveloped by the love of his devoted family.

Standing in the presence of a man struggling to stay connected to reality can be a jarring experience, but it is a reminder as well of the infinite dignity of human beings endowed with God's Spirit, for no loss of cognitive function can lessen this indomitable force. Alzheimer's disease is considered a family disease, as the emotional effects of the decline it precipitates are felt not only by the diagnosed, but by those who care for them as well. Though the suffering of Christ is everywhere apparent in these individuals, we must remember that God is infinitely good, and that all He wills for us is for our greater good. We must keep in mind that we are called to accept and do God's will, and nothing can separate us from the love of Jesus, not even an illness that seems to rob patients of their cognitive gifts. As a physician, I see in such patients not tragedy but opportunities to minister to brothers and sisters in Christ with an attitude of mercy and grace, while reminding them of His steadfast love. With this consideration in mind, though Alzheimer's may remain an incurable and at times overwhelmingly difficult disease with which to cope, we may embrace a faithful hope, confident that our present and future is in God's hands.

Skilled Nursing Facilities

I began my internship in 1976, following my completion of the final three years of clinical sciences studies in the hospital. Gone were the days of arriving at a set time in the morning, putting in one's hours, and leaving in the evening. Now I was on call, and spending nearly every waking moment practicing medicine. It was exhilarating and deeply satisfying, but also demanding to such a degree that I spent very little time at home, often sleeping at the hospital instead.

One day I thought to break the monotony, so I devised a plan to take my mother out to eat. She had grown accustomed to seeing me only briefly, as I would make quick stops at the house to pick up a change of clothes, then dash back to the hospital. This time would be different, though. I would take her away with me for dinner. *But it is just dinner,* you might say—why would that require a plan? The fact is eating out was not normal for us, and if I did not find a way to trick my mother into coming along, she would find a dozen reasons to refuse. "Why should you pay for dinner, when I can make it at home?" "I'm not dressed properly to go out." "It's too expensive." I could hear all the objections play out in my head before even setting out to pick her up. I knew that I would need to catch her off-guard and give her no chance to decline.

Our house was only a short distance from the hospital, so I arrived there quickly, darting excitedly into the house and asking my mom to get in the still-running car. The questions came, of course— "Why? Where are we going? How can I leave when I'm dressed like this?"—but I was ready for all of them. "Don't worry about any of that," I told her. "Just come out to the car with me, please." She reluctantly agreed, trusting that I would not be up to anything sinister, but wondering, no doubt, what this could be about. Was I about to deliver some earth-shaking news to her?

Perhaps she was relieved as we pulled into the parking lot of the rotisserie chicken restaurant. Where surprises are concerned, this was a relatively tame one, after all. I had no life-changing revelations for her—only dinner. The restaurant was a no-frills, old-fashioned carhop, where you place your order and the food is brought to your car on trays that hang from your windows. There, in the comfort of our old Toyota station wagon, my mother and I enjoyed a decent chicken dinner and a beautiful conversation. We touched down on everything from my work to my sisters to how she and my father had been doing. In short, we did some much-needed catching up, and as I saw her safely back home, I began to understand how special those two hours had been for us both. It was so much more than dinner; it was a chance for us to freely share with each other our intimate feelings—to laugh together at the joys of life, to voice our regrets, our hopes, and our gratitude. And, indeed, as I made the short drive back to the hospital to finish my day, I could not have been more grateful to call her my mother.

Sometimes all it takes is a surprise visit or even a phone call out of the blue to brighten a person's day. I see proof of this time and again as I visit patients in skilled nursing facilities (SNFs). Most such patients are over the age of 70 and face physical limitations of some sort. As extended periods of time spent alone in bed can be quite mentally taxing, I find that these patients are always happy to see me, receiving me with great enthusiasm and warmth.

I enjoy visiting my patients in the SNFs, so I go personally, rather than asking a colleague to do so. While I tend to these patients, their experiences keep me grounded and in check with what it is really important in life. Witnessing their suffering, struggles, limitations, and gradual physical and mental deterioration makes me more aware of my own human condition and how blessed I am with the gift of my vocation as a doctor caring for others.

I am careful to remind myself that we all are children of our heavenly Father—that because we are created to his image and likeness, we all have an intrinsic and transcendent value, regardless of our appearance, skin color, ethnic origin, mother tongue, education level, religion, position in society, and the state of our soul—in grace or in sin. No matter who they are, what they have, and what they do, each of these patients is a unique and unrepeatable person in the eyes of God, as they are His creation, and there is an undeniable value to each patient's life. I accept these patients as they are, and help them in their particular circumstances, without complaining or making a judgment.

This task requires patience, as I must take the time to listen to what is important to these patients—not necessarily what is medically important to me regarding their conditions. I must meet with their relatives who frequently voice complaints and opinions regarding the care of their loved ones. I go to battle with patients' health insurance companies when the providers will not approve a longer patient stay. Often, there is bountiful paperwork one must complete to get a vital medication or device for a patient. At times I must even argue with ambulance companies so patients may be transferred to the right hospital for further care.

It is to be expected, then, that through my years of caring for these patients, I have at times felt sad, discouraged, and frustrated because I could not do better for them or more for them. That said, there were also many times when I felt truly gratified when my patients were discharged home, thanks to the concerted efforts of the nurses, vocational nurses, medical assistants, therapists, and administrators working at the SNFs. And for the few patients for whom recovery was not possible, I helped them to accept the ends of their lives.

The spiritual wellness of my patients is part of a comprehensive recovery plan, so as always, I inquire and respect their religious beliefs. I encouraged them to enhance their relationship with the Good Lord by praying, reading the Bible, and attending religious services when available at the SNFs. Occasionally, in the company of my wife, I distribute Holy Communion to some Catholic patients who requested the Eucharist from one week to the next.

I was acquainted with one such patient, *Martha* for more than 24 years. She suffered from heart disease, irregular heartbeats, obstructive lung disease, recurrent pneumonia, and severe low back pain from compression fractures of the lumbar spine. Martha also had a permanent pacemaker. Her condition was aggravated because of shingles, involving her left anterior chest wall with severe neuralgia. She was a devoted Catholic and mother of two, who prayed the rosary and lived bedridden for several years at a local SNF, before she died at age 84.

Denise, my patient for 25 years, also comes to mind. She and her husband were practicing Catholics, whose only daughter died of an analgesic and sedatives overdose in her early thirties. She had multiple medical conditions that kept her in the hospital for long periods of time. Denise underwent several abdominal and spinal surgeries, and had heart and lung disease, in addition to diabetes and low production of red and white cells. Her low back pain was so severe that she used a battery-operated device to deliver morphine directly into her spinal canal. She was able to receive Holy Communion as a resident at a local SNF, but remained in bed most of the time.

I think, too, of *Landon,* my patient of 27 years. Landon is a proud father of three daughters and two sons. He has had diabetes for many years, and coronary artery disease that required the deployment of stents. After retiring, Landon was not able to take care of himself, so he moved into a SNF, where he has stayed for the last five years. In general, he has been stable, but occasionally he is hospitalized for acute medical conditions. He likes to listen to old Spanish songs, and is able to keep up with group activities in his circle of friends. Landon prays every day, keeps his Catholic paraphernalia in his room, and receives Holy Communion every time he has a chance.

Growing old is an inescapable facet of human life, but not one we need fear or resent. Though my trips to SNFs at times provide me with a sobering reminder of what we shall all become if, God willing, we should live to advanced ages, they also offer refreshing opportunities to tend to a most vulnerable population. Sometimes one finds that it is not strict medical care SNF patients require, but merely a friendly smile and a cheerful greeting. As parents who cared for their sons and daughters when they were most vulnerable, so should they in turn be cared for in their twilight years.

Do not cast me off in the time of my old age;
do not forsake me when my strength is spent.
— Psalm 71:9

The Unschooled

Sometimes the greatest lessons in life come from the most unlikely of sources. They comprise an education gleaned not from books, professors, or even our wise and respected family elders, but from the experience of living life itself.

My own life has been largely academic, as I took an early interest in learning and later found myself having to meet various scholastic requirements in order to continue advancing through my studies. This process of having to make the grade began well in advance of my university years. In Peru at that time, progressing to high school was not automatic. Space in the public high school system was limited, so young people looking to continue with their education were forced to compete with one another academically. I remember my father explaining to me at the age of 12 that he did not have the money to send me to a private high school, so I would either have to apply and qualify to attend a public high school or become a *peon*, slaving away full-time in the candle factory—powerful motivation to keep on top of my studies, indeed! I studied hard, and secured a spot at Sanchez Carrion public high school.

In later years, I would again need to work hard and apply myself academically, in order to obtain a government-sponsored scholarship to study at Peru's National University of Trujillo, School of Medicine. Still later I was fortunate enough to receive my post-graduate education in the best universities and medical centers of the Midwest. This exposure to some of the country's greatest medical minds did wonderful things for me as a budding physician, but also led me to the assumption that everyone who is born in the United States is inherently able to read and write.

And then I met *Daniel*.

Daniel was a 54-year-old, hardworking, well-built man, who first visited my office about five years after its opening in 1993. I got to know Daniel as I was caring for his elderly mother. His father had died at age 82 of complications from diabetes and heart disease. Daniel was the oldest son in the family, with one sister and seven brothers, two of whom had passed away by the time of our meeting. In time, Daniel's wife and all of his surviving siblings would become my patients as well.

Daniel was not what one might call a model patient. He suffered from a number of medical conditions prevalent in his family history, including high blood pressure, high cholesterol, diabetes mellitus, heart disease, irregular heartbeats, and heart failure, but he did not seem to fully appreciate the severity of these medical conditions, despite my many admonitions. Furthermore, he demonstrated a susceptibility to the opinions of his relatives and friends, bouncing from doctor to doctor and trying new diets, medications, and treatments, one after another. Daniel was also inconsistent with his appointments, at times missing scheduled visits, and at other times arriving unannounced. He often failed to take his medications as instructed, as well. Caring for such a patient requires unwavering patience and perseverance, and I was always happy to oblige Daniel, but as his well-being was at all times of the utmost priority to me, I did wish he would adhere to my instructions.

Around the year 2000, Daniel brought me a document to complete for his temporary disability. Ordinarily patients present these applications to me with their personal information filled out, leaving me to complete the areas reserved for physicians, but upon flipping through Daniel's forms, I noticed his sections had been left entirely blank. I wondered at this for a moment, and then suddenly an unspoken understanding was formed between us: Daniel was illiterate. I felt immediately humbled, as I had believed I had been doing a good job caring for Daniel, all the while not realizing that his inability to read may have played a decisive role in his non-compliance with my instructions for taking his medications.

Daniel became visibly ashamed as I realized he could not read or write. He expected, perhaps, that I would question his intelligence or treat him differently than before. On the contrary, following this understanding, I began explaining his ailments by using heart models, listing his medications on a table with instructions for taking them with or without meals, and writing numbers and drawings on the labels of each of his medication bottles. In addition, I was careful to repeat for him in detail the reason(s) for taking the medications and the instructions for their use. I am happy to report that these simple measures helped Daniel learn the nature of his conditions and attend to his office visits and the administration of his medications more carefully.

As I came to know Daniel better, I learned that he had attended elementary school, but had always found it difficult to comprehend sentences. Daniel's teachers advanced him from one grade to the next, despite his demonstrating very little improvement in his ability to read and write. Daniel's father was also illiterate, and separated from the family when Daniel was 15 years-old. At that point, Daniel began to work, and gave his whole paycheck to his mother, who was educated and took care of Daniel's personal and financial affairs for years. His brothers, except for one, also had elementary-level educations, were illiterate, and failed to complete high school. Daniel's only sister, who lived with their grandmother and grew up under very different circumstances, was the sole sibling with a college degree.

I recognized Jesus in the face and life of Daniel, whose illiteracy had rendered him a marginalized person in our society, with a low self-esteem and feelings of inadequacy. As a person who cannot read, he is insecure and suspicious of others who try to help him. I viewed my encounters with Daniel as opportunities to care for a man in need of help, both as a physician and as a Catholic whose calling it is to serve without expectation of reciprocity. Indeed, my greatest reward was feeling that I had always done my best to tend to his and his family's needs for many years.

I would like to believe that Daniel learned from our interactions to be more trusting of people who would care for him. I, too, learned from our time together. I was reminded that some of the most important lessons in life—humility, patience, empathy, compassion and tolerance—are best learned through human interaction. Books and teachers are undeniably valuable sources of information, but there is life-knowledge to be gained from everyone around us, if one will but look. In this way, the young may teach the old, meek may teach the brave, and, indeed, a day laborer may teach a physician.

Difficult as such encounters with patients uneducated in English can be, they are more challenging still with patients for whom English is a second language, as many such patients are also unable to read and write in their native tongues.

In our practice, a handful of patients are unable to read or write their native language of Spanish. This presents significant disadvantages in their ability to understand essential information, and may also result in low self-esteem, anxiety, and most commonly the misuse of medications. Special measures must be taken to ensure that such patients understand their medical conditions and the correct use of their medications.

I think now of *Betty*, an octogenarian Spanish-speaking lady with a long history of diabetes mellitus, heart disease, and chest discomfort (angina pectoris). Betty was born on a farm in a rural area of Mexico where there was no school to attend. Upon arriving in Los Angeles in 1958, Betty began working two consecutive shifts to make ends meet. Today she lives with her only married daughter, who is unable to bring her to her office appointments or help her as much as Betty wishes.

For more than 26 years, Betty has taken two buses to come to our office—a long journey made considerably longer if she arrives late to a bus stop. Nonetheless, she is consistent with her office visits and medication use, and her medical conditions remain stable.

Betty is a simple and honest woman, who remained hard-working until her retirement at age 65. Because we share the same native language, Betty is able to communicate clearly with me, and she trusts my medical advice. That said, she has admitted to feeling frustrated because of her inability to read and write the language, particularly when she receives mail from Medicare. She knows the documents are important, but because she cannot interpret their meaning, she is left feeling helpless. Furthermore, Betty feels vulnerable to people who would take advantage of her on account of her limitations as a non-English speaker. She is an American by naturalization, but still feels as though she is a second-class citizen.

Throughout the many years I have treated Betty, she has brought most of her Medicare correspondence to me so that I may explain it to her. This uneasy situation inevitably creates anxiety, as rumors on

Spanish television stations have led her to believe she is at constant risk of losing her health insurance and other federal or state benefits.

"Doctor Caceres, in one week I have received five documents from Medicare," she explained to me on one occasion. *"I don't understand them. Nobody in my family has time to help me with these papers. I am afraid the government will take my Medicare and/or Medical away from me."*

Betty did, indeed, receive five different documents, in five different envelopes, on a total of twenty-one sheets of paper. All the above documents were in English, with some containing additional pages in Spanish. Included in the documents are phone numbers for language and translation services available to non-English-speaking patients. The paperwork also explains a patient's right to contact his/her social worker for more information—a resource ultimately unavailable to Betty, as she could not recall the name of the worker handling her case. Given the circumstances, Betty and I agreed that the best course of action would be for her to return to my office the next day and meet with a member of my staff who was well-versed in Medicare paperwork and could walk her through it.

I am sorry to say that such scenarios with patients feeling their health benefits are in jeopardy are not uncommon. It is customary for Medicare to send letters printed in English to recipients, providing them with a breakdown of previous office visits, tests, and other services they received. These standard reminders often become a source of great anxiety for patients who are unable to read them, as the recipients wrongly believe the documents are warning them of an impending cancellation of their Medicare health benefits.

Through these encounters with my illiterate patients, I am reminded of Jesus preaching, loving, and caring for the uneducated

and marginalized people of his time and our time. His love and compassion toward people who suffer goes so far that he identifies himself
with them:

> *"I was naked and you gave me clothing, I was sick
> and took care of me, I was in prison and you
> visited me."* — *Mt 25:36*

I view these illiterate patients as my brothers and sisters in Christ,
with unique limitations. They have shared with me their feelings of
inadequacy, frustration, shame, confusion, helplessness, anxiety, and
alienation, extending far and beyond their physical medical conditions. I am eager and passionate to dedicate extra time and effort to
help them during each office visit in every way I am able. These
patients are special in the sense that they require more attention to
address their hardships than the average patient. By being present
for them, listening to them, and showing my true concern and
respect, I would like to believe I have not only contributed to improving their physical health, but inspired them to greater spiritual vitality as well.

Kidney Transplants

During the final year of my internship, I received word that Clara—one of two sisters who had moved to the United States—would be returning home for a visit. Clara had found success abroad, working as a nurse in California, and I reveled at the chance to catch up with her in person. After all, she had made it in the United States of America, which had always been something of a magical place to us as kids. It was where all the great movies and magazines came from. The best medical textbooks, too, were printed first in the States, and we in Peru would receive translated copies some three years later. I wanted to hear stories about Clara's time in California, of course, but it was the idea of spending time with her that excited me the most, for we had always been particularly close as siblings, and I admired her greatly for her compassion and her generosity.

That generosity would catch me quite by surprise and indeed change the course of my life forever. Early into her visit, Clara told my father she would like to petition for one of her siblings to come to the United States. Clara herself had become a citizen through naturalization, and wanted to extend the opportunity to one of us living in Peru. My father suggested that she choose me, and a short time later we were on our way to the American Embassy in Lima to file the necessary paperwork.

Many life-changing events then happened in succession in the following year of 1978. In January, I completed my civil service and received my M.D. degree from the National University of Trujillo,

School of Medicine. The following month, I began studying for my medical exams, and completed the interviews for my residency in the United States. Finally, at the end of August the same year, I made my way to sunny Southern California to live with Clara and her two boys.

Now, I had made it to the States, but one significant hurdle remained: I really could not speak English. I had learned to read English long before, excitedly flipping through copies of Time magazine with my sisters in our youth, but the only speaking I had ever done was limited to schoolroom English classes, which were rudimentary at best. I wasted no time trying to remedy this, traveling to Cypress College with my sister and enrolling in English as a Second Language (ESL) classes on the very day of my arrival in the country. The classes cost only $7 per semester at the time, and afforded me access to the school library, where I would study for the TOEFL (Test of English as a Foreign Language) as well as review for my medical exams.

The library of Cypress College was unlike any other I had seen before. Indeed, its vastness and seemingly endless inventory formed a theme that would repeat itself again and again as I saw more of the country. Supermarkets the size of museums gushed with an infinite variety of offerings. Cars for as long as one could see zipped across well-ordered streets and highways so plentiful it seemed nothing was but a short drive away. It is one thing to see these things in pictures and in daydreams as a child, but another thing altogether to take in the sights and smells and sounds in person. I was a stranger in a strange land, and it was exciting beyond description.

Of course, I could not let myself be overwhelmed by my new surroundings, as I had many responsibilities. In addition to spending time at school, which ran Monday through Friday from roughly 6am to 7pm, I was helping to care for my two nephews. Cooking was not a skill I had acquired growing up, and my early adventures into preparing meals for the boys are probably something we would all prefer to forget. Nonetheless, I did my best to help with any work that needed to be done around the house, while practicing my English every opportunity I got.

This included purchasing a small black and white television for around $100. Color TVs were out of my price range, but it was the audio that mattered most to me anyway. Rosa, the other of my two sisters who had come to the States, advised me to watch as much TV as possible, explaining that eventually I would come to understand what was being said. This did turn out to be helpful for my English comprehension, but the one-sided nature of the medium meant I was not getting a lot of practice speaking the language. I realized I would need a good deal more time to become fluent in conversation.

To help make ends meet, I found a temporary job working for $2.70 an hour as a medical assistant in a facility for the mentally challenged. A short time later, I upgraded to $6.00 an hour, working at Fairview State Hospital. Good fortune and naïveté contributed to my obtaining the position, as I rather innocently circumvented the hiring process and called the CEO of the hospital directly—he was listed in the phone book. I had impressed him with what must have appeared as brashness, and he graciously arranged a position for me.

Four months into my stay in America, and just as I was beginning to grow accustomed to my new life, I received a call from Peru. Celia had died, they said. My mother was gone. It had happened suddenly and unexpectedly. I was thunderstruck. Less than half a year had passed since the 50th anniversary celebration, where she had looked joyous and full of life. Now she was gone. Worse still, financial restraints prevented me from returning to Peru in time for the funeral services, which are traditionally held with great immediacy. I found my consolation in prayer and the recollection of a thousand beautiful memories of my mother.

Staying busy, too, was helpful, and in the following years I would pass the Educational Commission for Foreign Medical Graduates (ECFMG) Examination and the Federal Licensing Examination (FLEX), allowing me to begin the application process for a medical residency in the United States. The timing of my completing the exams was such that I had missed the chance to apply locally that year, but there were two to three remaining positions in the Midwest and the East Coast. I applied to each, and prayed earnestly to Jesus, that he might help me to continue on my path of ministering to the sick.

Each day I waited eagerly in anticipation of a response, and at last a single school contacted me. The University of Illinois had a single position available for a Family Medicine resident, and said they would like me to interview. So, fingers crossed, I set off for Peoria.

When I arrived for my interview on the seventh floor of a tall medical center building, I felt again like a stranger in a strange land, only not for the vastness of the campus. It was, in fact, a picture on the wall that inspired these feelings, and even drove me to consider returning to the elevator and leaving altogether. Pictured within the frame were some 100 residents with faces and names that were nothing like my own. "What would they want with a doctor who began his career in a remote part of South America?" I wondered. Nonetheless, I decided to go through with the interview, to better know how to handle them in the future.

I was interviewed by at least six doctors and a handful of residents. As well as I believed I had performed, it still did not occur to me that I would have any chance of obtaining the position, until Dr.

Neuhoff, the Chairman of the Family Medicine Department and one of the senior doctors on the panel, revealed to me that he would be voting for me. Dr. Neuhoff had kindly offered to drive me back to the airport, and delivered this news to me before I left, with the admonishment that his vote alone would not secure me the spot—several other panelists would need to concur. Knowing that I had stood out to even one doctor offered me a ray of hope to which I would cling in the agonizing weeks that followed as I waited anxiously for the call that would determine where my future was to lie.

And by the grace of God, the news that came was good. Against tremendous odds, I had been accepted to the only program for which I had interviewed. So, on June 20, 1981, I began my Family Medicine residency.

It is hard to imagine how different a course my life might have taken, had the university phoned me with a denial. It seemed at the time as though being accepted was of life or death importance. Of course, when I reflect on it today, I realize that, important though it might have been to me at the time, the call was far from critical. What if every moment of every day really were so vital, though? Suppose life itself hinged on a single incoming phone call. For some 94,000 men and women awaiting kidney transplants in the United States each year, this is more than a supposition—it is a reality.

I think now of *Abel*, a 38-year-old patient with a history of long-standing hypertension; hypertensive heart disease; diabetes mellitus; and end-stage renal disease, requiring hemodialysis three times per week. Abel received a mechanical aortic valve replacement in 2011, and required multiple medications, including warfarin, a blood thinner used to avoid clots from forming in the new valve. At the time of our meeting, Abel had been on a kidney transplant list at a local university hospital for six years.

A married man with no children, Abel was humble and simple, with a strong faith in God. His fellowship with Jesus was very apparent, as he read the Bible, prayed, and attended church services regularly. As Abel anxiously awaited his kidney transplant, he experienced a profound conversion through his unconventional but genuine prayer. He began to accept each moment of the day as an opportunity to live his life to the fullest, rather than living in sorrow and asking, "Why me?"

Over the course of many years, Abel continued on hemodialysis, enduring numerous tests and hospitalizations due to infections, diastolic heart failure, and diabetes. He was young, but exasperated by his inability to carry on a normal life as his peers could. He waited patiently in anticipation of that life-changing call, and then one day in July of 2017, it came. Abel was then granted a renal transplant from an unrelated donor. Soon after the surgery, however, he developed recurrent multiple clots in the abdomen and other complications, in part because of anticoagulation medications. Thankfully, this was brought under control, and has since been cared for by other physicians. I am happy to report that Abel is still doing well at the time of this writing.

I think, too, of *Jerry*, my patient of roughly 18 years. For a long period of time, Jerry did not have health insurance, and paid for our services as a private patient at lower fees. He was a non-practicing Catholic, divorced twice, and had a kind heart and a desire to help people. Jerry worked as a real estate agent, and specialized in helping Hispanic clients find and purchase their dream homes.

Jerry came to me with arterial hypertension, diabetes mellitus, and high cholesterol. He had to pay out-of-pocket for his medications, and we did our best to provide him with samples. Unfortunately, because his conditions were not usually associated with symptoms, he did not take these medications on a regular basis. Neither did he follow my orders for blood tests.

Several years passed, and I did not see Jerry at all. Much had changed when he returned to us. He was now 64-years-old and had developed new diseases, as well as severe complications related to the medical conditions for which I had previously treated him. He had survived a heart attack and developed narrowing of the coronary arteries that wrap around the heart, requiring multiple stents (flexible tubes made of wire mesh) to keep them open. His heart function was reduced, with inability of the heart muscle to pump blood, which we refer to clinically as heart failure.

Jerry had also developed severe kidney failure, requiring hemodialysis three times a week, for over three years. For two years, his name had been on a kidney transplant list at a hospital in another county. Early in 2017, he was inexplicably removed from this list, despite having a relative willing to donate her kidney to him.

Jerry underwent the required pre-kidney transplant evaluations in my office and at a local hospital. He had severe hardening of the arteries of his heart and was not a candidate for any further procedures or heart surgery. He was treated with optimal medical therapy, and his heart function markedly improved. Jerry was a candidate for enhanced external counter pulsation (EECP) therapy, but this was ultimately not possible because of an arteriovenous fistula (abnormal connection between an artery and a vein, surgically created for hemodialysis) in his left thigh. Jerry also had peripheral artery disease in both legs, and complained of a recurrent painful left shoulder, requiring steroid injections. He was referred to the nearby university medical center for consideration for a kidney transplant, and after a few weeks, he was on the waiting list.

Despite his failing health, Jerry continued working part-time and enjoying time with his fiancée, with whom he lived. He had been married twice before, and had a teenaged son in another state. Over the years, Jerry had developed a growing personal relationship with our Lord Jesus, and made a habit of praying every morning when he got up at 4 am, before his hemodialysis, as well as every night. Jerry learned to trust Jesus and leave in his hands the future of the kidney transplant that he had long been awaiting. He read passages from the New Testament and the books *Rediscover Jesus* and *Resisting Happiness*. I can form a clear image in my mind of Jerry praying for himself and with his children, as his health deteriorated.

I recognized Jerry as a person with a constant awareness of his illness, limitations, and aspirations for a second opportunity in life, as he grew wiser, got closer to Jesus, and became better attuned to the things that really mattered in his life. He lived with a persistent preoccupation for a kidney transplant to become a reality as soon as possible. He knew that he had done his part, and could do nothing more than wait for that most important call.

I witnessed Jerry's frustrations, mood changes, family problems, financial hardships, and physical limitations, as he became unable to work for more than a few hours each day at his demanding real estate job. Remarkably, however, even as Jerry's body became progressively more fatigued and broken-down, his spirit never showed the slightest signs of breaking. He persevered in earnest hope of the transplant he dearly needed.

Unfortunately, in early October 2017, Jerry developed edema in the left ankle and foot. We ruled out the presence of a deep vein clot in the lower extremities. He continued taking his medications as directed, but died suddenly at the side of his bed at around 4 am in the second week of October, while preparing to go to dialysis. I believe Jerry neither wanted nor anticipated a sudden death, but, as he shared with me, he was content to leave his life in God's hands. May he rest in peace.

I often contemplate what it must have been like for Jerry to await a kidney transplant for over 2 years. His cycle of hemodialysis three times a week was a time-consuming routine that made it difficult for him to fulfill his activities at work and at home, but it also gave him a sense of security and control over his kidney failure, while he awaited a transplant. This prospect of a life-saving organ transplant brought with it a sense of insecurity, too, however, as he had no influence over his fate, and was resigned to simply wait patiently for a call that could well come too late. Indeed, as I write this, there are more than 94,000 patients waiting for a kidney transplant, and only slightly more than 16,000 such surgeries are performed each year. The long-term emotional tension and anxiety a candidate must face while waiting for a new kidney—to say nothing of life's usually daily stressors—lie at the center of existence for these patients. How terribly difficult it must be to not merely accept such a reality but to overcome it on a daily basis, gathering the will to wait patiently for a life-or-death call that may never come.

In view of the composure that transplant patients like Abel and Jerry must demonstrate as they await life-changing operations, it seems altogether silly to ascribe even a modicum of frustration to traffic jams and long supermarket lines. Patience for such individuals awaiting transplants is more than a virtue; it is a tool necessary for survival. It is a skill that must be gained to maintain one's mental health in the face of failing physical health. Above all, it is a measure of character from which the more fortunate can draw valuable lessons in faith and humility,

> "...*knowing that suffering produces endurance, and endurance produces character, and character produces hope.*" — *Romans 5:3-4*

The Ill-Favored

A few months into my Family Medicine residency in Illinois, staff in the Internal Medicine department suggested to me that I should consider transfer to the Internal Medicine Residency Program. Because it had always been my intention to specialize in Internal Medicine, I took the opportunity at once. All the while, I continued to improve my English, carrying a pocket dictionary in my coat to ensure that there were no errors in my charts. After a few months, I would no longer need the little book, but I continued to work independently on my English pronunciation.

The ability to speak the language clearly was a necessity, not only for patient interactions, but for the grand rounds in which I was required to participate. The grand rounds system is a form of weekly medical education wherein one lecturer must present a medical condition and treatment to an audience of doctors, residents, and medical students. These presentations were taken very seriously, and required weeks of preparation that included research, scriptwriting, and coordinating with the medical center's audio-visual department to prepare slides. I would then take the additional step of rehearsing my lectures multiple times in front of a willing medical student, who would closely monitor my dialogue for pronunciation errors. In time, this strategy would earn me a reputation among the residents for delivering excellent presentations—a flattering if unnecessary distinction for one who derived such joy from the act of teaching.

As I continued in my residency, I found myself increasingly in the company of cardiologists—even on my days off—and all the while more interested in the heart. So, as the end of my residency drew near, I interviewed with 13 cardiology programs scattered about the Midwest. The cardiologists with whom I had become so well acquainted were kind enough to write letters and make phone calls on my behalf, and I was accepted to all 13 programs. I went with my first choice—Washington University in St. Louis, Missouri.

In 1984, I began my clinical cardiology fellowship at Washington University, commencing what was to become a period of intense productivity and travel in my life. When the fellowship concluded in 1986, I headed to Mount Sinai Medical Center at the University of Wisconsin in Milwaukee to undertake another fellowship in cardiac electrophysiology. When that program concluded, I remained at the university for an additional year, working as an instructor of medicine and publishing my first medical papers. I was subsequently offered another teaching position, this time in North Carolina at East Carolina University, as an assistant professor of cardiac electrophysiology, where I remained for a year and continued to publish academic papers. I would then be recruited in 1989 by Atlanta South Cardiology Associates in East Point, Georgia, for the purpose of establishing a cardiac electrophysiology laboratory at South Fulton Hospital. There I enjoyed a very productive year, conducting more than 260 electrophysiology tests and starting a relationship with a charming young nurse named Fe.

By 1991, I felt as though I had acquired sufficient experience in medicine, academics, and in life itself to explore opening my own practice. I returned to Southern California to be nearer to my sisters, and took a job with the Saint Louis Medical Group, working from 8am to 5pm for income. After work, I would attend a night class at UCLA, to learn how to start and operate a small business. Then, at last, in February of 1993, I opened Caceres Medical Clinic in La Palma, California, to fulfill my promise to myself and to God: I would offer the highest possible quality of care to all those in need.

All those in need. Upholding this oath with conviction is something that remains vitally important to me to this day.

There have been numerous occasions on which I have received requests from patients and skilled nursing facilities, asking me to take care of new patients because their primary care providers and/or specialists, for whatever reason, were no longer interested in taking care of them. Even in my own practice, there were a handful of patients that my colleagues preferred not to see when they arrived at our office. For me personally, though, these seemingly undesirable and challenging patients are precisely the ones I have always sought to care for.

The first time I saw *Wilma*, she was in a stretcher with her son by her side. She arrived by ambulance from a nursing home. At age 74, she suffered a stroke with right hemiplegia. She was unable to speak, and had a gastrostomy feeding tube. She needed a long overdue heart evaluation because of multiple cardiovascular conditions, including systolic heart failure, irregular heartbeats, a pacemaker, and fluid around her heart. Though chronically ill and depressed, she found some relief as we communicated in Spanish and I caressed her forehead before she left. On subsequent visits to my office in which we conducted noninvasive testing, I was able to adjust Wilma's medications and significantly improve her condition. Today, I am happy to report that she is 80-years-old and doing quite well.

Another patient who comes to mind is *Theresa*. The only daughter of a Central American couple who emigrated to the States because of civil unrest in their native country, Theresa married at only 14-years-old. After the birthday of her second son, she was diagnosed with schizophrenia, a serious mental disorder involving abnormal thoughts and behavior that impair one's ability to perform daily functions. She received treatment for this condition, and a few years later, she gave birth to her final child. Theresa's spouse and her children were very supportive of her.

I had been Theresa's mother's physician for more than 18 years when, at the recommendation of her husband, Theresa became my patient. Theresa's husband explained to me that, under her current treatment plan, her condition was not improving at all. Indeed, her behavior was highly erratic: she would wake up in the middle of the night and start cooking for no apparent purpose, she would get in and out of bed throughout the day, and she frequently gave money and other possessions to friends with no recollection of having done so. Hoping in earnest that I would have some answer for his ailing wife, Theresa's loving husband would drive her more than 55 miles once a month to visit my office. I am happy to report that making some modifications to her medical regimen did, in fact, help Theresa. Of course, given the late stage of her illness, Theresa could not be completely cured, but she was able to resume normal daily activities with only a single medication. Theresa was always very polite and appreciative for every small thing our health team did for her. Unfortunately, she died recently of natural causes.

I think also of *Alice*, who was 42-years-old when she came to see me for the first time. Alice was disabled, on social security, and living by herself. She had two children from whom she was estranged. Alice often presented with complaints of a most bizarre nature, requesting, for example, a wheelchair to move around the office, despite having no physical limitations. I vividly recall an instance in which I entered the exam room to find Alice lying down on the examination table on her side. Then, quite before I could so much as greet her, she launched into an extensive monologue, explaining that she had been to see multiple specialists who concluded that she is in dire condition, she is now homeless and must move to a hotel or nursing home at once, that she has been robbed, that she lost her medications, and that I must write a letter on her behalf to an unnamed organization. Where shall one start?

Alice was eventually diagnosed with bipolar affective disorder, but she refused to take the medications ordered by her psychiatrist. Now, at 57, she expresses a litany of complaints, from transient loss of consciousness and postural tone to chest pain, neck pain, lumbago, and scabies, among others. She demands that I refer her to multiple specialists, insisting that she will take matters into her own hands if I do not comply. Unsurprisingly, the battery of tests Alice has undergone, including MRIs of every part of her body, have all produced unremarkable results.

Despite her distinctive demeanor, Alice has been our patient for more than 17 years, and we accept her as she is. She is aware that we are ready to help her as much as we can, and counts on us to care for her without judgment. She "knows her rights," as she says, and periodically uses the federal and state health system to her advantage. She is certainly not a patient my staff and I will soon forget.

"My daughter needs a medical certificate of her mental disabilities to apply for citizenship, but the psychiatrist she has been seeing for more than four years has refused to do it, despite multiple requests. Can you help me?" This was the request of *Maria*, my patient of more than 7 years.

When I met Maria, she was a single mother, looking after her 42-year-old daughter, who lost her father tragically at the age of 16. Maria's daughter had bipolar disorder, and had been taking medications prescribed by her attending physician for several years. She also had diabetes and mild heart disease. Because of her mental disability, she was unable to learn the English language to a level necessary to pass her naturalization exams. In response to the above request, I filled out a six page document declaring a medical basis for her daughter's exemption from such a requirement. I am happy to report that Maria's daughter is now 47, an American citizen, and medically stable.

I think also of *Ivan*, a patient with cerebral palsy and paralysis in the lower half of his body. Ivan was first brought to me by his parents (also my patients), at age 39, in a special wheelchair. I deeply regret that it appeared that his previous doctor was no longer willing to take care of him. This had understandably caused Ivan to become agitated, as he needed refills for his medications and cardiac clearance for dental work. Ivan's sporadic noise making, moaning, and erratic motions of his face and arms did not in any way interfere with or change the bedside manner of my staff. He was seen and taken care of with respect and compassion. Because Ivan was living at home with his parents, we referred him to a home health nursing agency for further care.

It was very straightforward to recognize Jesus in the faces of the above patients, as I realized their innocence and goodness in spite of dealing with matters beyond their control. It brought back memories of my time working in a facility for the mentally challenged a few months after I arrived in the States. Indeed, Jesus is not always revealed to us in the places and with the people we expect; rather, he is revealed to us in the most unlikely places and in the most unlikely people. These encounters helped me to think about the things that really matter in life, and provided me with reassurance to continue working to help others.

Pope Francis, in echoing the sentiments of his predecessor Pope John Paul II, reminded us that every human life, "unique and unrepeatable, valuable in and of itself, constitutes an inestimable worth." Such life "that we are called to protect and defend is not an abstract concept, but is always manifested in a flesh and blood person: the newly-conceived child, a poor marginalized person, a sick person suffering from discouragement or a terminal illness, a person who has lost their job and cannot find work, a refugee or ghettoized migrant...life manifests itself concretely in people." These powerful words and the underpinnings of my strong Catholic faith call upon me to serve all patients who seek my help. Patients whose needs require of one extra energy and patience should not be made to feel burdensome. Rather, they must be shown a special degree of compassion. In this way, something more than a mere transactional relationship is established between doctor and patient, and I am rewarded for my time, my patience, and indeed my faith, in inestimably fulfilling ways.

Marriage

The process of building a medical practice from the ground up is not an easy one. The small business management course I had taken at UCLA had helped me to formulate a business plan, but a good deal more work would be required to turn that plan into reality. How blessed I was to have the invaluable support of my fiancée Fe, who helped with every step of the process.

Before anything, we would need to find a location for the office. The first consideration was the rent, which would need to fit our modest budget. Secondly, the area should not be saturated with doctors; we were looking to find a location where a doctor was needed. To this end, we took out a large map of the city of Cypress and its surrounding areas, and placed pins on it to represent the offices of every local doctor. We were fortunate enough to locate a building for lease in a shopping center in one of the pin-free zones. It was perfect for our needs, and we wasted no time securing it.

Staffing the office was a very simple matter: I would be the doctor, of course, Fe would be the nurse and x-ray technician, and I would hire an employee to function as receptionist as biller—a three person operation.

We opened our doors on February 11, 1993. Around the same time, I had the good fortune of encountering a first-rate accountant whose office shared a parking lot with ours. He projected that we would recover our investment after two months in operation. He was right.

Two months later, on June 19, Fe and I were married. The modest wedding reception was elevated to a thing of true beauty by the presence of relatives who traveled to the country for the occasion: the mother of my lovely bride from the Philippines, and my sisters Bita and Lucy from Peru. I cannot overstate the bliss I felt on this day and the honeymoon that followed—events eclipsed only by the births of our sons Joseph and Steven, in 1994 and 1996 respectively.

In the nearly three decades that have followed, Fe has remained my faithful companion and a devoted mother to our two boys. A look back to our early days together punctuates for me how much simpler times were back then. Now, we live in an unprecedented time where conversations are conducted from behind the screens of monitors and smart devices, relative strangers from half a world away are labeled "friends" on social media platforms, and couples are even going on "virtual dates." The difference is astounding.

With marriage on a steady decline here in the United States and many countries abroad, I must say it is refreshing to have among my patient load at least six couples with exceptionally long-lasting marriages. These committed spouses have graciously over the years shared with me their joys, their struggles, and their fellowship with the Lord that, like glue, has held them together as husbands and wives for more than 60 years each.

Larry and Lily

Larry and *Lily* became my patients in 1993. The couple was wed just one week before the attack on Pearl Harbor, and Larry, who served in the United States Army, was honorably discharged after WWII ended. After trying several jobs without much success, Larry decided, with Lily's blessing, to join the US Air-Force, where he served until his retirement in 1965. The couple had two sons and one daughter, the younger son remaining my patient until he passed away at the age of 46, after several years of mental illness and cardiac arrhythmias.

Larry was a soft-spoken, old fashioned American gentleman, and strong-willed Lily was his "Princess." Larry had an extensive history of high blood pressure, heart disease, high cholesterol, prostate disorders, and arthritis. An angiogram revealed a severe blockage of more than 90% in the proximal third of the artery that runs in front of his heart, placing him at high risk to have a massive heart attack. Despite this, he refused bypass grafting surgery or coronary angioplasty. He was treated with therapeutic life changes, medications, and enhanced external counter pulsation, a non-invasive, non-surgical treatment designed to reduce episodes of angina. Larry was a low-keyed man who would patiently read books while waiting to be seen at my office.

Lily, who was in every way as polite as Larry, was by contrast considerably more outgoing in nature. She was very fond of talking about her children and grandchildren, for whom she had a palpable love. Her medical conditions were not severe, but she developed diastolic heart failure and edema in both legs. Like her husband, she was punctual with her arrangements for medical testing and doctor's visits. She was compliant with her medications as well, and would carry them in a large and heavy handbag with a hodgepodge of items ranging from scissors to cookies and anything in between.

After 67 years of marriage, Larry passed away in 2009 at the age of 89, and Lily died two years later at age 88. I saw in them a caring couple who remained loving and kind to each other for 67 years, believing in and practicing the American values and Christian virtues that helped them to persevere in their unconditional love and commitment to each other. Although they did not attend church services on a regular basis, there is no question they were living according to the greatest commandment. Indeed, their youngest daughter remembers both as devoted and Christian parents, committed to helping others.

Robert and Beth

Robert was born in Iowa in 1938. When he was four years old, the family moved to Wisconsin, where he would attend a small school with the same teacher until the 8th grade, before moving on to high school. Robert worked hard from a young age, rising at 4 am to milk cows on the family farm. He would then study from 8 in the morning until 3 in the afternoon, before returning to his duties on the farm until late evening. In 1957, after his high school graduation, he joined the Marine Corps in San Diego. There he worked as a radio operator in the amphibious unit for three years.

Beth was born in 1940 in California. She was already engaged when she met Robert. In 1958, Robert, in his marine uniform, accompanied Beth to her prom. They were married in October of the same year. After Beth's graduation, she got a job in the Sears warehouse. Then, in January 1960, Robert finished his assignment with the Marines. He immediately procured a job at North American Aviation (later known as Rockwell International), starting at the bottom with a compensation of $ 1.99 per hour. He remained there for 33 years, until his retirement in February 1993.

Robert and Beth's first daughter was born in September 1960. The labor and cesarean section delivery were complicated, and Beth was in a coma for three days. The couple was told that they would need to sacrifice the baby in order for Beth to have a chance to live, but that did not prove necessary. In later years, Robert and Beth would reflect on this event as their first miracle, as both mother and daughter survived free of any complications. The couple went on to have two more daughters, born in 1962 and 1966 respectively.

While Robert continued working at Rockwell International and moving upward in his job, Beth dedicated all her time to raising her three daughters. She was a very active mother indeed, for many years juggling Girl Scouts meetings with school and sports events, until the time came for the children to go away to college. The family enjoyed the outdoors, and would frequently vacation in a 34-foot recreational vehicle on weekends and summers.

In 1981, Robert became gravely ill and underwent an 18 inch resection of his colon due to a malignant tumor. He had a recurrence of the cancer the following year, and was successfully treated with radiation therapy for six weeks. He has since become the longest survival of colon cancer in my practice.

Over the last 10 years, I have been privileged to witness firsthand Robert and Beth's loving care and dedication for each other and their children. The family has had its share of medical scares, their oldest daughter, too, having colon cancer that was successfully removed and cured. Beth had multiple medical conditions which required surgeries, frequent hospitalizations, and recovery in skilled nursing facilities. Her diabetes and hypertension resulted in chronic kidney disease, requiring hemodialysis three times per week. Because of her condition, she uses a wheelchair and special transportation.

It has thus fallen on Robert to care for her devotedly at all times. Fatigue, frustration, and depression have all touched Beth throughout the process, but with the help of her family and God's grace she has been able to overcome all these trials and difficulties.

Although Robert and Beth do not attend a particular church, they have a relationship with Jesus Christ and consider themselves Christians. In Beth's words, "I have The Lord in my heart, I pray to him, and read the Bible and the books you gave me." The couple has been married for more than 60 years, and Jesus has been the true link that has kept them together. They have cared for others less fortunate, inviting, for example, a 59-year-old stroke victim to their home for Thanksgiving and Christmas dinners. They have been blessed by the Lord at all times, and they are ready to meet Him any time they are called.

Imagine living together with the same person for more than 60 years. It seems that these couples were successful in their marriages because each spouse did his or her part to love and respect the other. Their long and healthy marriages are a result of their commitment to each other in a bound that is perpetual and exclusive "until death do us part." For them, love is not just a word or a feeling, but a decision to care with honesty, trust, and patience for and to each other selflessly and ceaselessly. These couples appear to have found God in the events of their lives. In a world where couples have taken up more liberal and detached ways of living, honor, love, and commitment to each other remain of paramount importance to Lily, Larry, Beth, and Robert. I have watched these couples work through the very best and worst of times, discussing challenges with one another, praying together, and enduring though not always easy solutions to their troubles. I myself have learned from their example; without their intention, these six couples have helped me to become a better husband. In the end, I have realized above all that faith and fellowship with Jesus—as these couples lived in accordance to God's greatest commandment—was the very backbone of their marriages and the agent of their longevity.

Cigarette Addiction

In time, Caceres Medical Clinic became Caceres Medical Group. We had accrued a faithful patient base, and I had taken on additional staff to help with our growing operation. The increasing number of patients seeing me for heart-related issues prompted the creation of Buena Park Heart Center in 1994. Here we would create comprehensive heart care programs for patients, tailored to their individual cardiovascular conditions.

We proudly carried on in our humble little corner of La Palma Avenue and Valley View, until at last, in 2002, our accountant, who had by then become a dear and trusted friend, advised us that the time had come to find a larger building. I had long followed a policy of reinvesting the fruits of our labor into higher quality diagnostic equipment, office maintenance, and anything else I believed would better serve my patients, but these efforts were at times somewhat bottlenecked by the meager size of our operating space. Finding a new location and building a medical center to my own specifications presented me with a dream opportunity to serve my patients, and on August 1, 2004, that dream came true.

Our new, two-story building offered over 14,000 square feet of operating space. We fitted it with state-of-the-art diagnostic equipment, including cutting-edge x-ray, ultrasound, echocardiogram, stress echocardiogram, and electrocardiogram machines. These, in conjunction with our excellent staff, would allow us to bring a new level of care to our patients.

There were, of course, some setbacks.

It is natural that in the course of nearly three decades of business one would encounter some unscrupulous characters. A doctor, for example, who was released for not meeting our performance standards, filed a complaint with the labor board of California. He manufactured a number of grievances, claiming that he was not allowed to take breaks and was forced to work overtime. Similarly, a receptionist, who was reassigned to a position in a different department for the same pay, became disgruntled and filed a discrimination suit against the practice. When this proved unfruitful, she filed a subsequent claim for sexual harassment. Most disheartening of all, though, was the near-repeat of the same event, in which a failed discrimination case was turned to a sexual harassment case, but involved the plaintiff attempting to bribe employees to corroborate her story.

All of the above-mentioned claims were unsubstantiated and ultimately unsuccessful in leeching money from us, but that is not to say that they did no damage. Fighting those allegations took a tremendous toll on my physical, mental, emotional, and even spiritual well-being. And though I knew that with God as my witness I had committed no wrongdoing, still I became anxious, lost sleep, and began to stress eat. I tried through prayer, self-reflection, and even professional counseling to think positively, to be less anxious, to be happier.

In time, I was indeed able to return to a state of stable overall health.

Niccolo Machiavelli once famously wrote that "Where the willingness is great, the difficulties cannot be great," suggesting that with the proper amount of willpower, any adversity can be mitigated or altogether eliminated. It is the sort of adage that holds up better in print than in practical application, for we know that there are certain struggles that cannot be overcome by sheer force of will. We also know that the proper amount of determination to conquer the challenges at hand is not something that can simply be summoned at any given moment. Some struggles, like cigarette addiction, can constitute lifelong battles in which the limits of one's determination are tested on a daily basis. Finding the will to quit smoking can quite literally amount to choosing life over death. When framed this way, it may be all too easy for non-smokers to say the choice is simple, but for nearly a billion smokers the world over, it is indeed the very furthest thing from simple.

I am reminded of *John,* who first visited my office in 1993. I vividly recall the end of our first encounter, as he said to me casually, "By the way, my wife wants me to tell you that over the last few weeks I have been having chest pain." John was known to have hypertension and high cholesterol. Further cardiac testing revealed severe hardening of the coronary arteries, requiring coronary bypass surgery. At the time I met John, he was smoking about 20 cigarettes per day. His prostate had already been removed, and he had recurrent urinary tract infections from using a catheter to empty his bladder, at the suggestion of his urologist. In the years that followed, John continued smoking every day. He worked at a railroad company, but lived an otherwise sedentary life, playing with his computer, and/or lying on the couch watching TV. As a result, his medical conditions grew worse over time.

Despite optimal tolerable medical therapy; John had angina pectoris (chest pain), had several coronary angioplasties, and developed heart failure. His attendance to his scheduled appointments was erratic, but thankfully he did come when he was in immediate need of our services. Toward the end of my time as John's physician, he developed lung cancer, with an unusual amount of fluid around the lung (pleural effusion). He was placed on hospice care, and I continued as his physician, visiting him at home. Eventually, he died peacefully, surrounded by his wife and grandchildren.

Over the years, I came to learn more about John, and really grew to appreciate him. One of a physician's greatest frustrations is when his patients fail to appear for much-needed follow-up visits—and John did this frequently—but I accepted and genuinely cared for him. I saw him struggle with his work, his illnesses, and the notion of getting old. He could not seem to overcome his cigarette addiction, nor could he modify his sedentary lifestyle. In spite of his struggles, John never whined about his medical conditions, but instead accepted his diagnosis. During a visit to my office, he shared how he had fallen in love and gotten married for the third time. He would faithfully take this wife on vacation out of state every summer. John also cared for his mother of 94 years of age, to whom he was very important, and who worried deeply for him, as he was her only living child. I remember John as an honest person, a caring dad, and a loving grandfather.

When I reflect on my time with John, I feel that I failed in helping him quit smoking permanently. He was not a practicing Christian, and I never tried hard enough to talk to him about Jesus and His effect on my life. Instead, I merely handed Christian literature to John, believing the rest would simply fall into place. In retrospect, I realize that I was more interested in helping his body than his soul. I felt inadequate, and I did not know how to contribute to his mental and spiritual health, which could have aided him significantly in his battle against cigarette addiction. To this day, I feel as though I missed a vital opportunity to do better for him.

I also think of *Travis*, who first came to my office in 1993. Like John, he worked as an engineer for a railroad company. He was married and had 3 children. He also smoked heavily for many years, and suffered from hypertension, hyperlipidemia, and severe hardening of the three coronary arteries. He would eventually develop severe chronic obstructive lung disease—a disorder that persistently obstructs bronchial airflow—and undergo coronary artery bypass surgery.

For the most part, Travis was compliant with his appointments and medications. Gradually, his obstructive lung disease deteriorated and his shortness of breath on exertion, and even at rest, worsened. He tried to quit smoking multiple times without success. His nicotine addiction was stronger than his will to quit.

I clearly remember the day I explained to Travis that if he continued smoking, he would one day have to carry a portable oxygen tank to perform common activities like taking his grandchildren for a meal at a local restaurant. Unfortunately, this precise scenario would later come to pass.

Travis was hospitalized with recurrent pneumonia several times. Shortly after his retirement, he developed respiratory failure, requiring an incision on the anterior aspect of the neck and opening a direct airway through the trachea, using continuous oxygen 24/7 to keep him alive. Eventually, he went home with a breathing machine. I would visit him at his home, to check on his condition. Two days before Christmas in 2012, I visited him with my two sons. We sang a couple of Christmas carols around his bed and prayed for him. Five weeks later, he passed away.

I encountered Jesus in the life of Travis, as he suffered because of his ailments to the point where it was difficult for him to finish a sentence without gasping for air. He also bore great internal suffering on account of the physical and mental disabilities of his grandson, who, at the age of two, had accidentally swallowed his mother's sleeping pills. Despite having received medical treatment, the child developed chronic neurological and corporal incapacities, requiring special care 24 hours a day. Eventually, the boy had to be placed permanently in a special medical facility.

Travis was looking forward to enjoying his retirement. He used to ask me how much longer he would live. Sadly, it was to be a life cut short. I learned to appreciate his life, his love for his family, and the frustrations he felt on account of his declining health. His memory still lives in all of us who had the privilege of meeting him. Today, I remain the physician of his wife and son.

I began wondering, *what else might I do for patients like John and Travis to help rid them of their smoking addictions?* Both had tried behavioral counseling, nicotine replacement therapy, read literature on quitting, and other measures, none of which yielded long-lasting tobacco cessation. Doubts remain in me, as does a certain feeling of liability, as I think that I may not have done enough for them in this regard. This can be very difficult for a physician to accept. As surely they must have, I feel sad and powerless, for I view cigarette smoking as an addiction almost impossible to overcome in the absence of extreme willpower. Regrettably, both John and Travis died of the complications related to their addictions to cigarettes. Though I am convinced that I respected, loved, and served John and Travis to the best of my abilities, I cannot help but wish that they had found the will to break from their addictions, perhaps not with the simplicity of Machiavelli's ideal, but with the grace of God, for, as we are told in Matthew 19:26, "...with God, all things are possible."

Heart Failure

In 1977, a German-born doctor named Andreas Gruentzig performed the first coronary angioplasty procedure in Switzerland. I was in the second year of my internship, and would never have guessed that this profound medical breakthrough of using a balloon to open up arteries would one day become a procedure I performed regularly myself. Less than a decade later would come the stent, a coil of wire mesh that bolsters the walls of arteries and prevents them from narrowing again. These two major advancements, along with coronary artery bypass grafting surgery and various medications, continue to save countless lives.

After several years in practice, I began to recognize some trends among patients with coronary artery disease. Many required repeat angioplasties and stents every few years. For others, limitations in daily living remained, even after surgery and in spite of taking the best medications available. This prompted me to investigate whether there were alternate treatment modalities available to help these patients whose quality of life had become so terribly poor. It was then that I discovered enhanced external counter pulsation (EECP), a safe and non-invasive treatment with clinically proven benefits for angina patients.

In EECP, pneumatic cuffs—similar to the kind placed over your arm to check your blood pressure—are placed around the lower extremities and made to inflate during the heart's resting phase. This inflation squeezes blood vessels and pushes blood back to the heart muscle, opening partially closed coronary arteries and improving circulation to the heart. This fascinating method of treatment was not available at the time I underwent cardiology training, but the clinical studies I reviewed upon learning of it were so compelling to me that I began providing the therapy to my patients in 2007. Since then, we have seen remarkable quality of life improvements in patients with recurrent angina for whom there seemed to be no hope.

I am always on the lookout for new and clinically proven treatment methods for my patients, particularly when their conditions severely impact their daily lives. It is commonly known that heart disease is the leading cause of death in the United States, but lesser known are the debilitating symptoms with which its sufferers must contend while alive.

I think now of *Adrian*, a diesel mechanic referred to me for evaluation and treatment of his heart disease. In 2006, he suffered two heart attacks with considerable heart muscle damage, leading to heart failure—impaired contractility of the main pumping chamber of the heart. This resulted in shortness of breath on exertion, easy fatigue, lack of energy, dizziness, and palpitations, among other symptoms. Over the next several years, he had several procedures to keep the arteries of his heart open, and an ICD (device able to perform cardioversion, defibrillation, and pacing of the heart) was implanted. At this point, he was incapable of performing his routine work as desired, he became permanently disabled, and subsequently lost his healthcare insurance.

Adrian was the father of four sons and one daughter. Two years after his first heart attack, Adrian's youngest son, at age seven, underwent his first kidney transplant. Then, after more than 24 years of marriage, Adrian abandoned his wife and children, moved to a neighboring state, marrying and supporting a new wife and her children. Adrian was everything to his only daughter, age 19, who was devastated when

Adrian left home. It was she who encouraged her mom to file for child support a few years later after Adrian left his family.

After his wife of twenty-two years passed away, Adrian moved back to California. Since then, his daughter has been caring for him with unparalleled dedication, and it was she who brought him to my office in 2017. He had had previous lumbar surgeries, hypertension, diabetes mellitus with long term use of insulin, hyperlipidemia, and worsening heart failure. His medications were updated accordingly, he underwent more coronary angioplasties, and received 35 sessions of enhanced external counter pulsation therapy—a treatment to improve the circulation of his heart. In early 2018, his ICD generator was replaced, and in February of 2019, he underwent a double coronary artery bypass grafting surgery. He was critically ill, developed an irregular heart rhythm, and was transferred to another university hospital. For 45 days, his only daughter remained next to him day and night in the hospitals. Eventually, his heart failure improved, and he recovered with optimal tolerable medical therapy. However, we kept monitoring the moderate to severe narrowing of his neck (carotid) arteries associated with previous "small" strokes, and his partial blindness as result of his diabetes.

By early 2020, his youngest son, now 29-years-old, underwent his second kidney transplant. Adrian's personality subsequently changed, and he became verbally abusive to his daughter, sometimes throwing his food to the floor and shouting at her in a violent manner. Adrian grew tired of living with his daughter, who was assisting in her brother's recovery. One day, he abruptly left his daughter and son, moving to a hotel with a homeless friend. He wanted to be by himself, moving around with no restrictions as his conditions required, and playing the drums in the choir of his Catholic parish. Since then, he has been living alone and coming to his appointments by himself.

It has been a heartbreaking experience for me to witness Adrian's tumultuous recovery from severe heart failure and to see the damage that was done to him as a child reflected onto his own daughter and son. It would seem that he cares only for himself and not at all for his children. Indeed, his daughter resents the fact that Adrian neglected his original family, leaving them to dedicate his life and resources to his second wife and her children. At this point, Adrian is medically stable, with shortness of breath on mild exertion and fatigue, but he needs a caregiver to supervise his compliance in taking 14 different medications per day, as well as to attend his appointments with different providers and assist with other activities of daily living.

Adrian has assured me that he reads the Bible, attends mass regularly, participates in the church choir, and prays. Sadly, it would seem that he lives with double standards, with contradictions between his relationship with the Lord and those with his children.

I think also of *Norman*. At the age of 44, Norman was driving home from a birthday party with his wife on a Sunday morning in August of 1995, when suddenly he felt a crushing pressure in the middle of his chest. The chest discomfort began to worsen, radiating to his left arm, he became short of breath. He barely made it to a hospital near his house, and he was seen by the emergency room physician. A few hours later, I was with Norman in the ICU. He was having a massive heart attack due to complete blockage of the artery in front of his heart, resulting in a large amount of heart damage. There was no cardiac catheterization suite in the hospital, so Norman was treated medically. A few days later, he underwent a triple coronary artery bypass grafting surgery in another facility.

Norman, an accountant, soon realized that he was unable to run his office as before. Indeed, the healed infarct had resulted in a large scarred area in the anterior wall of his heart, becoming thin and bulging out (aneurysm) with each beat. He developed congestive systolic heart failure with profound fatigue, shortness of breath, lack of energy, recurrent chest pain (angina) and palpitations in performing activities of daily living. His ejection fraction (EF) was 15% (normal is 50-80%), which means that 15 percent of the total amount of blood in the left ventricle was pushed out with each heartbeat. Thus, Norman was referred to Stanford Medical Center, the Cleveland Clinic Foundation, and the University of California Los Angeles (UCLA), where he was placed on the list for heart transplantation around January of 1996. Needless to say, he was receiving the best tolerable optimal medical therapy.

The subsequent years were extremely difficult for Norman. At that time of his heart attack, he had a son and a daughter of 14- and 8-years-old respectively. He underwent multiple cardiac testing and procedures and saw his heart failure cardiologists frequently at UCLA and in Cleveland. He was aware of his very poor prognosis, as most patients in his condition die in two to three years. He was anxious, depressed, and living with the uncertainty of having a high likelihood of dying while waiting for a heart transplant. In addition, although he was partially disabled, he had to work and face with courage the daily challenges of his office work. In the meantime, in November of 1998 at the Cleveland Clinic, he underwent a left ventricular reconstructive surgery (Modified Dor Procedure), in which the operator removed the scarred bulging anterior area of the main pumping chamber of the heart to return it to a more normal shape to improve his heart failure. . The procedure was successful, and his EF increased to about 25%. To his knowledge, he is the only survivor of this surgical procedure, which is no longer done as often as before. The other 400 patients or so either had a heart transplant or have already passed away.

Norman went on to have more angioplasties to keep his coronary arteries open. His heart failure gradually improved to a point that, since 2002, he has been considered temporarily unsuitable for heart transplant. However, heart rhythm disorders (arrhythmias) caused by abnormal electrical signals in the upper and lower chambers of the heart were documented. In October of 2003, he received an ICD. This small battery-powered device implanted in his chest wall, like a permanent pacemaker, detects any life-threatening rapid heartbeats, and can deliver electric shocks via one or more wires connected to the heart to fix an abnormal rhythm. Since then, Norman has received several appropriate jolts as well as improper ones due to paroxysmal irregular beats from the upper chamber of his heart (atrial fibrillation).

The eldest son in a family of three, Norman lost his father to stomach cancer when he was a teenager. He became the support of the family, working and studying until he got his university degree before emigrating to the United States because, among other reasons, Christians were relented and persecuted in his country of origin. Norman is a Christian orthodox with a strong faith in God and unconditional love for his family. He attends Sunday congregations regularly. He continued to look after his mother until she passed away in 1999. Norman learned to live with the real limitations of his heart failure, continuing to work at his office for long hours sometimes, and taking naps between clients if needed, to recharge his batteries so to speak. He developed medically refractory ongoing chest pressure (angina pectoris) and was placed on a brand new expensive medication by 2007, which he could afford only for a few months.

Norman's heart condition improved further with the arrival of a new medication in July of 2015, which was supplied by the Heart Failure Program at UCLA. The combination of sacubitril-valsartan helped Norman to lower the risk of being hospitalized when symptoms worsened, as well as lower the risk of death from heart failure. Indeed, in October 2017, a nuclear medicine study revealed an EF of 41 percent, and no evidence of significant restriction of blood flow to his heart (ischemia). Since then, Norman has had four more non-cardiac surgical operations with fine results. Currently, he is still working about 40 hours a week, taking his 14 daily medications, walking every day as tolerated, and keeping his appointments with me and his cardiologists at UCLA and Cleveland Clinic—not bad at all for a 69-year-old gentleman who was once enlisted for heart transplant 24 years ago. That said, unusual fatigue, shortness of breath on mild exertion, and occasional angina pectoris are real limitations to Norman's daily activities. He lives with an awareness of his heart and other medical conditions, but his attitude remains a positive one, as his full trust lies in Jesus.

Norman's outliving of his initial prognosis by more than 24 years happened by a confluence of God's good grace and advanced medical technology. Adrian, too, was the fortunate beneficiary of divine grace and medical breakthroughs, without which he would certainly have been lost. This intersection of human ingenuity and Providence represents but one of the infinite ways in which we are helped by God to help one another. I am time and again reminded of my own good fortune to work as a vessel of healing, harnessing the innovations of science with a modest God-given ability to serve my fellow man and thereby serve our Lord.

The Club of the Nineties

In her convocation address to Howard University's class of 1998, Hillary Clinton offered the following admonishment to the young graduates: *Don't confuse having a career with having a life.* Her goal was to impress on her audience the notion that some of the greatest rewards and accomplishments in life lie outside the workplace. This is a principle of which I believe most of us are cognizant, but too often the demands of the workplace leave us without the time and energy to pursue outside interests. Finding a proper work-life balance can be a near-Sisyphean task, and one with which I myself admittedly contend on a daily basis.

The merits of being deeply devoted to one's work go without saying, but these can come at the cost of sometimes much-needed leisure pursuits. In my own life, I am able to mitigate this to a degree by having hobbies connected to medicine. For example, outside of office hours, when I am not working in the capacity of a doctor, I very much enjoy studying medicine. My fascination with the field has never wavered throughout the years, due in part to the tireless work of research scientists and biomedical engineers who continue to advance the field of medicine with new discoveries and technologies particularly in cardiology. I am still very fond of teaching medicine, too, and I devote a portion of my free time to conducting presentations, seminars, and lectures for my staff and fellow physicians. I continue to write and publish medical articles, as well.

Because my Catholic faith is central to my life, the majority of my non-medical pursuits are focused on learning and exploring my faith more deeply through books and other media. I am an avid collector of DVDs that examine a wide variety of religious topics, and I have an extensive assortment of spoken-word CDs as well. My study is brimming with books written by everyone from laymen to leading theologians, whose unique perspectives and insight challenge and enrich me in equal measure.

In truth, I have more media than I can digest, given that I am still on the full-time schedule of a doctor. Time constraints also preclude me from taking up new hobbies, like learning to play the piano and improving my typing skills. I'd also like to travel, both domestically and internationally, and explore various charitable pursuits. And perhaps one of these days I might allow myself to just spend a lazy day at home doing nothing—if only to see what all the fuss is about!

Though my bucket list is long, I feel no special sense of urgency to begin checking things off it. By the grace of God, I have managed to maintain my own health such that I can continue to serve my patients, and that remains my priority and indeed my joy. Of course, the day will come when I must step back from my duties as a physician, and when that does happen, I will at last have the time and, God willing, the energy to devote to other interests.

My assurance comes not merely from my own good health, but from a roster of very long-lived patients I have had the pleasure of caring for over the past 27 years. Many of them have lived well past the age of 90, and with the help of strong family support, have shared a finesse and positivity that were truly inspirational to me.

One such patient who comes to mind is *Juliet*. Juliet married an army officer who served in WWII and was discharged with honors.

The couple had 4 daughters. Juliet's husband, too, was my patient for some time, until his death from complications due to Alzheimer's disease in 2001. As one would expect of a 93-year-old, Juliet had multiple medical conditions herself, from arterial hypertension to osteoarthritis in multiple joints. Dementia, on the hand, she did not have. Indeed, she was intellectually sharp, closely following her health and family affairs and promptly voicing her opinions of national and local government matters. Juliet usually visited my office on a monthly basis, and would solve puzzles while waiting to be seen. She was always aware of her complaints and what she expected to be done by her primary care providers and specialists. This was familiar territory for her, given that she had worked in a hospital for more than 35 years before her retirement in 1998. When Juliet turned 90 in 2015, I celebrated the event alongside her closest friends and family.

Unfortunately, Juliet had been poorly advised to discontinue having mammograms after age 80. In early 2018, she presented with a painful right breast mass which turned out to be breast cancer, spreading to her lungs and possibly to her brain. Several years prior, she had endured the death of her oldest daughter from the same disease. Juliet was placed in hospice, and I had the opportunity to visit her home with my wife. Despite her weakness, she was still charming and hospitable. A few weeks after our visit, she died.

Juliet was a Christian lady of solid faith, who taught her children by example how to live according to God's standards and not the world's standards. As her health deteriorated, she never expressed resentment or voiced complaints. She accepted the present and the moments of her life without fear, instead placing trust in her maker. She kept her good sense of humor and her smile until the very end.

92-year-old *Pearl* is the oldest of 11 children. She came to the States about 14 years ago, after her husband was murdered in her native country. She lives with her youngest daughter and her family. She has hypertension, irregular heartbeats, heart failure, chronic obstructive pulmonary disease, and urinary incontinence. A joyful and vibrant lady who walks with a cane, Pearl is courteous and rarely without a smile on her face. She faithfully maintains her appointments and takes her medications. Despite her medical conditions, Pearl is overall in good shape, particularly compared to other women in her age range.

Pearl is a simple and content person who practices the best rule for the spiritual life, as she receives and accepts, moment by moment, whatever God sends her. Her oldest daughter died of a cerebrovascular accident, and her son of diabetes complications. In spite of these tragedies, Pearl's unshakable faith and positive attitude have made it possible for her to live peacefully and free of worries, with total trust in God, "until He takes me to heaven." Pearl prays every day, attends mass regularly, and recites the rosary every night with her family, "for all the good and bad people who also need God."

It is my habit to give Catholic books as gifts around the Christmas season, and Pearl has shared her enjoyment of these books with me, reporting that they have helped her to grow in her spiritual life and strengthen her friendship with Jesus. She keeps our patient information brochure in her purse, and whenever she has the chance, she proudly shows the picture of her doctor to her relatives and friends. Though it is not her outright intention, Pearl's captivating and contagious positive attitude serves as an invitation for us to all live life to the fullest.

Ivanna was a unique lady in her nineties, who wore hair rolls to bed each night, and meticulously did her makeup every morning. She was born with vitiligo—a patchy skin discoloration affecting many parts of her body, but took great pride in her appearance and looked younger than her stated age. As is common among women of her age, visits to the doctor represented a special event for Ivanna, a diversion from the daily monotony, and so she always wanted to look her best when she came to my office. This was especially important for her when I asked her to visit to participate in a "Club of the 90s" picture event. As Ivanna's oldest daughter says, "My mother was a simple humble person who was always self-conscious about her appearance."

The mother of three sons and three daughters, Ivanna arrived in California when she was 75-years-old. She was living with a daughter and granddaughter when she became my patient at the age of 88. Ivanna spent most of her life as a housewife, and never had the opportunity to attend school. In addition to vitiligo, Ivanna had other conditions, including thyroid and gastrointestinal conditions. She was 98 years old when she underwent a successful open surgical removal of gallstones at a local hospital.

Ivanna was an old-fashioned Catholic lady who liked to listen to the word of God and pray daily, attending mass every Sunday. She lost her husband to stomach cancer at the age of 100, and she, too, expired peacefully at home after her 100th birthday. Ivanna was a loving mother and grandmother who contentedly lived a life beautiful in its simplicity.

Bill is a 93-year-old gentleman who used to work as a truck driver and heavy equipment operator until his retirement. His neighbor of 30 years, my patient, brought him to see me about 20 years ago. Bill had multiple medical conditions, including diabetes, bilateral hip replacement, a permanent pacemaker, heart failure, cognitive impairment, and osteoarthritis in several joints. He used to be a very active, quiet and representative elder in his congregation as a Jehovah witness, until his wife died about 10 years ago. Now, without children of his own, he lives by himself. He cooks his own breakfast, but he goes out for lunch with one of his two neighbors who watch him daily. He spent most of the day watching TV and doing light house cleaning. Bill no longer reads the Bible, but continues to pray.

Bill has provided some challenges and opportunities for me to help, as I ordered and supervised the antibiotics given intravenously at his home for several days on different occasions, sending wound care nurses, physical therapists, and other medical services such as a hospital bed. I recognized Jesus in the face of this patient as a simple but wise person who accepts and lives moment by moment whatever God sends in his way without moaning.

Annie worked as a nurse for more than 35 years before arriving in L.A. in 1978. A single mother of five boys, she dedicated herself to her work and provided for them to the best of her abilities. To her dismay, not all of Annie's sons practiced her Christian faith, as taught. Nonetheless, she continued praying faithfully for them every day, begging the Lord for their conversion, which did indeed take place after 25 years.

Annie became my patient at the age of 71. She underwent open heart surgery, multiple total joint replacements, and other procedures successfully. Despite her medical conditions, and frequent trips to the hospital, today her mind remains remarkably clear for a 98 year-old. She loves to tell me stories about her days working as a nurse in her native land, helping people even outside of working hours, ready to assist friends and strangers when her services were needed, and so on. It is clear from Annie's stories—and indeed from her character—that her vocation as a nurse and her friendly relationship with the Lord have been crucial aspects of her daily life.

I had the opportunity to attend Annie's last two birthdays, and enjoyed the company of her five sons and extended family. She continues to visit my office regularly, as well. She walks with some difficulty using a walker and wears hearing aids, but has a good appetite and is at peace with herself, others, and God. She says she has been always blessed all her life, and she is ready to meet her Creator when she is called home.

The advanced ages of the above patients are impressive, to be sure, but more inspirational are the positive natures and collective joie de vivre they exhibit. After all, the blessing of longevity is lost on the joyless and the idle. With these things in mind, I await the opportunity to realize the promise of my own later years, if God should be so willing.

Temptations of the Flesh

In my view, complacency is something people of all vocations should endeavor to avoid at all costs, but in the medical world in particular, succumbing to the temptation to rest on one's laurels is not only irresponsible but potentially hazardous. A good physician's schooling is never really complete, as one must keep up-to-date with the latest developments in diagnosis, treatment, and many other facets of medicine. One must strive to avoid falling into mediocrity and staying married to outdated treatment methodologies that may be convenient for the physician, but not always ideal for the patient. This can mean putting in a tremendous amount of work—and at times investing a good deal of money as well—to stay on the cutting edge of quality care. It is terribly disheartening to me when I encounter private practitioners who fall to the appeal of doing what is merely serviceable to their patients.

But what of temptations of an altogether different kind?

A few months after I opened my practice in 1993, a patient in her early twenties came to see me for a routine physical examination without any specific new complaint. After I took her pertinent medical history, I handed her a standard cloth gown and asked her to put it on behind the semicircular curtain located in a corner of the examination room. Before I got the chance to turn around and reach the door, however, she promptly pulled down the long zipper of her dress, fully exposed herself, and exclaimed, "I'm ready!"

She was wearing transparent lingerie, and had ignored the gown entirely. I was taken quite by surprise by her behavior and intentions, but calmly explained that I would return shortly for the physical exam. Upon reentering the room some minutes later, I politely requested that she wear the gown, so I could proceed with the examination. I went on to order some basic blood tests for her, and she never returned to my office.

Cindy was a lady in her fifties, who became my patient around 1998. Later, she moved to Las Vegas, and a heart condition required check-ups with a specialist at a University Medical Center in Los Angeles every three months or so. She would therefore drive and stay in one of the hotels nearby to have her appointments with us as well. On one of those occasions, towards the end of my workday, she handed me a piece of paper with the address and room number of the hotel where she was staying, telling me, "I see you tonight." I was mute.

My first reaction was to call one of my friends in the priesthood and discuss the matter over the phone. He laughed, and said to me, something like this: "First, do not tell your wife. Second, next time, tell this lady that she is after the wrong guy, because you are married. Third, pray! And pray also for her." Of course, Cindy, like most of my patients, knew I was married and the father of two sons. It was not easy for me to avoid seeing her as a patient, as I was the only cardiologist in the practice. For a while, she was persistent and continued with her invitations, verbally and in writing, but eventually she stopped coming to my office.

Vicky was one of my first patients in 1993, who eventually died of complications from breast cancer. Once she died, her husband, Michael, in his sixties remarried a lady in her thirties. Michael had diabetes and erectile dysfunction, among other medical conditions.

His new wife became the head of the janitorial company that cleaned my office. She began expressing to me without provocation her marital woes and her daily dissatisfaction and frustrations with her husband. She voiced to me on multiple occasions her desperation for physical relations. I listened kindly and appeared ignorant to her advances. Because I was not her doctor, and was aware that she was a Christian, I suggested to her to establish a better friendship with Jesus through daily prayer, and to seek professional marriage counseling.

Another unusual experience was with *Christine*, a young single lady in her early thirties, who became my patient in 1994. Years later, on one occasion, she came to the office stating she had skin problems, immediately revealing her breasts, private areas, and buttocks, before I had a chance to ask her to put in a gown. On another occasion, she mentioned that what she needed is love, "someone to love me and sleep with me." I had known Christine for more than 26 years, and seen her transition from holding a well-paid job to becoming homeless living in her car. Now, at the age of sixty and after having multiple surgeries, we still have a transparent and caring patient-doctor relationship. Indeed, I have always treated her as a lady with much respect and consideration and as my sister in Christ.

Finally, there was *Myrna*, an employee of mine for five years, who upon moving to a new apartment, invited me to come and see her there, as she was submitting her new address and phone number for our records. She reiterated her invitations several times, but of course I never had the slightest desire to go. Then, as we opened the office one morning, she told me that she had dreamt about me the previous night, and would like to share the details of the dream with me later in the day. I discussed this situation with our office manager, who took disciplinary action in accordance with our employee manual. A few months later, Myrna was dismissed.

Thanks be to God that by his mercy and graces showered upon me, I was spared and did not fall down in these temptations of the flesh. I believe my routine of praying in the morning with my wife before leaving for daily mass at 6:30 am has helped me throughout all these years to keep my faith alive, trusting more deeply in God's grace than in my self-confidence. I do not think it is easy to overcome temptation, but it is certainly not impossible either, if we realize that we are not alone in this fight where good and evil are both present.

Clinical Depression

As the only boy among eight siblings, I did not have a big brother to look up to, but I did have many older sisters who offered me abundant love and inspiration. Indeed, I owe my coming to this country to my dear sister Clara, a nurse who could not have chosen a better vocation on which to focus her innate compassion and tenderness. She and I had a particularly close bond, so when she reported her breast cancer diagnosis to me in 1986, I was deeply saddened. Within two years, two more sisters, Margie and Lucy, would receive the same diagnosis. Each of them underwent surgery and appropriate medical treatment to achieve remission.

Unfortunately, Clara's cancer returned eight years later, this time with metastasis in the liver. She was treated at the best breast cancer center in Southern California, and received a bone marrow transplant and palliative care. As her primary attending physician, it was incredibly difficult to witness her deterioration firsthand, as she gradually weakened from the vibrant sister I once knew to a frail shell of her former self. She received hospice care until finally asking me to let her go with the Lord, and having her medications discontinued. Clara died peacefully in 1995.

Margie, too, a registered nurse would have her cancer return in 2002. She received a bone marrow transplant and further medical care at the same leading cancer center as Clara. Again I was present to witness the decline in her vitality and the heartbreaking image of a once dynamic woman now hairless and receiving a cocktail of medications through several intravenous lines. Though she remained in good spirits and showed some signs of recovery, she eventually succumbed to the disease in 2004, at the age of 56.

Lucy, a retired high school principal, received comprehensive treatment and fought her breast cancer for more than 10 years before dying at the age of 78 in 2009.

Regrettably, the list goes on. In 2014, my sister Vilma, an English professor, was also diagnosed with breast cancer. She was surgically treated, but refused to complete radiation and chemotherapy. In 2019, she developed metastasis in the brain, and continued to work until a few months before her passing at the age of 73 in early 2020.

My eldest sister, too, another registered nurse, would also battle the disease. Now 90 years of age, she is the lone survivor among 5 sisters who suffered from breast cancer.

While today I recognize that witnessing the painful struggles of my sisters has better equipped me to offer greater sympathy, understanding, and care to my cancer patients, participating in my siblings' care and sharing in their anguish over many years was quite harrowing for me. In a sense, I was forced to relive the same nightmare time and again, the agonies of the past reawakening with each successive incidence. Moments of hope would emerge from utter sadness, yielding again to a melancholy that at times threatened to affect my professional life. Thankfully, through prayer and the passage of time, I was able to overcome this sadness and restore an emotional balance to my life.

For individuals suffering from clinical depression, however, time does not heal all wounds. The road to becoming well-balanced and high-functioning individuals can be very long and fraught with uncertainty. To treat such patients, one must have a special level of compassion, patience, and foremostly a willingness to listen.

I think now of *Delma*, who was 28 years old when she came to see me in 1993, a few months after I opened my office. She suffered from hypertension, high cholesterol and obesity. She was married, had a one infant daughter, and was able to work full-time. Both of Delma's parents had diabetes, hypertension, and heart disease. Delma was not a devoted Christian, but like her parents, she was Baptist, prayed, and read the Bible on occasion. Everything would seem to have been going well for Delma and her family, until she was injured on the job and was placed on disability.

Now unable to work, Delma spent more time at home, put on more weight, exercised less, and dedicated herself to internet-related entertainment, so to speak. Eventually, her disability benefits expired, but after having lived a year in this manner, Delma had grown accustomed to a sedentary lifestyle. She lost interest in pursuing a more productive life or any form of self-improvement. Then she developed excessive hunger, fatigue, mood swings, agitation, apathy, and general discontent. She began to experience a persistent feeling of sadness and loss of interest. In short, Delma had become clinically depressed.

Delma was open to talking about her feelings with me, but initially resisted the help of a mental health professional. I encouraged her to reserve time for prayer every day, write in a journal, take daily walks, exercise, watch her calorie intake, attend her church services, and take an antidepressant medication. This plan appeared to be working for some time, but, as is so often the case, she lost her resolve, and despite employing many different coping skills—healthy and otherwise—she continued to experience multiple episodes of depression during her life.

Over the years, I came to know more about Delma's upbringing, her relationships, her ups and downs, her joys and sorrows, and her honest desire to know and love our Lord Jesus. I accepted Delma as she was, and did my very best to serve as her primary care provider and cardiologist. Occasionally, Delma and I would share quotations from the Gospels and remind each other we are children of God and we are loved unconditionally by our heavenly Father. These moments would reaffirm for me that, as God's children, regardless of our appearance, our skin color, our place of origin, our level of education, our religion, our position in society, and the state of our souls—in grace or in sin—patients like Delma are unique and valuable in the eyes of God, and it is my privilege to help them.

Delma did not drink alcohol or abuse illicit drugs; however she admitted that she and her husband would participate in swing parties in which couples in her inner circle would swap sexual partners. This resulted in a prolonged extramarital affair between Delma and one such swing partner, lasting several years. This adulterous situation gave rise to a devastating dispute with her husband, who eventually uncovered her infidelity and sought to have an affair of his own in recompense. I silently witnessed how Delma lived unhappily in this constant conflict between acting in accordance with God's commandments and following the desires of the flesh. As one might expect, this marital turmoil worsened Delma's depression. She began, even, to question whether it was worth continuing to live.

When Delma was around 42-years-old, she began complaining of premenopausal conditions, such as irregular and heavy menses, breast tenderness, weight gain, headaches, and palpitations. She was now morbidly obese, and became fixated on her appearance. So, on her own volition, she traveled to a town in Mexico, near the border, and she underwent liposuction (a body contouring procedure) in her upper arms, breasts, and abdomen. The wounds in the upper extremities and abdomen became infected, but this resolved after a few weeks of local treatment and antibiotics in our office. As expected, this was but a temporary fix to her body configuration, as she regained most of the weight loss achieved with liposuction within a few years.

Then, seemingly out of nowhere, Delma resolved to return to work. After some time on the job, her mood became pleasant and hopeful, and she discontinued her medications. But just as suddenly as she had taken it up, Delma quit her job for reasons that are not clear to me. She settled back into the same old jobless routine that had so troubled her before. Her physical ailments subsequently increased, and she developed hardening of her coronary arteries with angina pectoris and extra-heartbeats.

John, her husband, 3 years younger, lost his job and became disabled at age 45. Following a motorcycle accident, he acquired severe osteoarthritis in both knees and became addicted to narcotics. Meanwhile, Delma was diagnosed with multiple sclerosis, and gradually became less independent, because of muscle weakness, spasms, stiffness, difficulty walking, and dizziness. By this time, the couple was separated and residing in different counties: Delma was living with her 25-year-old daughter, and John was living with his sister. To make matters worse still, Delma lost both of her parents within one year, due to complications of diabetes and heart disease.

John, also my patient, finally underwent total bilateral knee replacement in 2016 when he was 48 years old, and Delma took care of him during the acute convalescent period. Then, in March of 2018, at the age of 52, a new diagnosis of diabetes mellitus with complications was given to Delma. The subsequent years were very difficult for her because she felt she was getting physically more limited, she was not able to drive as before and comply with her doctors' appointments, her husband was having an affair and this lady was harassing her on the phone, and she witnessed that her daughter was "getting tired of her" living in her condominium. In addition, because of her multiple sclerosis, she developed frequent urination and incontinence.

Given the circumstances, it was not surprising that Delma's clinical depression worsened, with bouts of excessive crying, apathy, hopelessness, and social isolation. Throughout our 27 year doctor-patient relationship, I have supported and encouraged her to depend more on God and less on herself, to read and reflect on the word of God, to lift her self-esteem, to take her medications and accept the help of a psychologist. One day, she told me that because of her current medical conditions, her situation at her daughter's home, and the problems with her husband, she wanted to die. Once again, I showed Delma how to use the tools to help her to overcome the negative feelings by meditation, prayer, writing in her journal, exercising, eating a healthy diet, sleeping at least 7 hours, and seeing a psychiatrist. Thanks be to God, Delma is still with us, trying to do God's will in her life, living one day at a time.

Though there is now plentiful clinically-sourced evidence to support the power of faith and spirituality in combating depression, it is—perhaps surprisingly—not from academia that I draw my recommendations to my patients. Rather, it is my own experiences that motivate me to encourage despondent patients to strengthen their relationships with God and their loved ones. For me, this meant attending mass daily, and praying in the morning and night. My wife Fe, too, was an invaluable source of love and support without whom my ability to overcome my sadness might not have been possible.

Faith, in whatever denomination one finds it, is a beacon with which to navigate even the darkest waters.

Educating Primary Care Providers

Ms. Sabina Nique and Mr. Nacarino Lavalle were my favorite teachers in elementary school and high school respectively. That, more than half a century later, I can still recall their names, faces, and indeed even much of what they taught me is less a compliment to my mind and more a testament to the powerful ways in which they inspired me. In my view, good teachers must do more than merely recite facts to their students. Good teachers instill in their students a drive to know more, to ask questions, and to continue exploring. Passion, too, is an invaluable quality for teachers.

My own passion for teaching manifested early, as I took great joy in helping fellow students work out math problems with chalk on the pavement of our elementary school. Later, I would channel this into a means of sustaining myself, tutoring high school students in the sciences. I continued teaching through medical school, as a resident and cardiology fellow, where I had the opportunity to help medical students and young physicians. Further on in my career, I offered conferences to my colleagues and wrote medical articles based on clinical research. In some of the aforementioned cases, teaching was a professional obligation, but my passion for it always rendered the act a joy, not a chore—something I approached with genuine enthusiasm, not discontent and a desire to simply get it out of the way.

When I started my private practice, I made the decision to conduct weekly teaching activities as a means of continuing medical education (CME). These instructional meetings continue to this day, and are mandatory for the primary care providers working with me.

I cannot overstate how gratifying it is to pass on knowledge to young men and women who are eager to learn. What follows are some accounts of the many wonderful opportunities with which I have been blessed to do just that.

> *"Had it not been for your help, I don't really think I would have gotten where I am now. Your excellent bedside manner was the best thing I learned from you."*

These were the flattering words of *Dulce,* who graduated as a medical doctor in the Philippines and practiced general medicine for two years before she arrived at California in the late 80s. She became a clinical lab scientist and worked in that capacity for roughly 10 years, while studying and eventually qualifying for a residency program in the United States. I have been personally acquainted with several foreign graduate physicians who were unable to pass these challenging examinations, and I admired Dulce's determination and willingness to prepare for them. She would often sacrifice leisure time on weekends and holidays in order to continue studying—a resolve that rewarded her with high test scores and fine professional prospects.

Beginning in 2002, Dulce spent two years under my supervision, applying her medical knowledge and sharpening her skills. We had one-on-one training throughout the day, involving everything from conducting physical examinations to clinical decision making for correct diagnosis and appropriate treatment. We reviewed patients' conditions, did weekly medical conferences with other physicians, and read current articles aimed at improving patient care. I discouraged her from pursuing a residency in pathology, and she decided to become a family medicine specialist, for which I wrote a well-deserved letter of recommendation.

She was accepted to start her residency in Family Medicine at the Texas A&M School of Medicine, where she finished in 2007. She practiced for 7 years in Texas and moved back to California, where she is now an Associate Program Director of Family Medicine in a large health system in Southern California. I was honored to be Dulce's mother's physician and cardiologist for 25 years, until she died recently at the age of 95.

Ace, too, comes to mind. Ace received his Bachelor of Science in Nursing in Manila, Philippines. In December 2011, he completed his Master of Science in Nursing at the California State University in Long Beach, California. In January 2012, he started his Optional Practical Training, as a Nurse Practitioner interning at my office, and we sponsored his working and permanent visa with the Department of Homeland Security. During that year, I taught and fully supervised Ace in his medical training as a new nurse practitioner graduate, in the areas of internal medicine and cardiology. He was able to learn the science and art of providing quality care to patients, listening to their concerns, and developing good clinical skills. He also learned from weekly conferences, attending one-on-one tutoring, and taking written examinations monthly. The end result was a comprehensive medical training with hands-on-experience that prepared him to become a competent nurse practitioner for years to come.

Ace remained at my office for more than six consecutive years, before leaving for greener pastures. But after two years of working for a different employer, he realized that the grass is not always greener on the other side. He then resumed working with me, focusing on internal medicine and cardiology, his preferred areas of practice. I have always displayed respect and consideration to my younger health workers, treating them as my colleagues in the medical field. I believe Ace's appreciation for this played a part in his returning to my practice.

Ace delivers individualized, quality care of the highest standard, with a compassionate attitude to patients, in the areas of adult medicine, geriatrics, and cardiology. He is an efficient and competent care provider who tends to the needs of all patients, and has a special bond with the Filipino community we serve. As I reflect on Ace's young career as his mentor, I can see how his mind, heart, and efforts are directed to those things that really matter in life. He is deeply devoted to his vocation as a healthcare provider, and endeavors each day to become the best professional he can be.

"The reason I got sick with ulcerative colitis is to get closer to Jesus, and now, having experienced being ill, I feel the need to help others, to have empathy...so, I decided to become a medical doctor to help others."

Edgar was born in Peru and arrived in California in 1990 when he was only four years old. While still in school, he attended classes in a local church, reading the Bible, memorizing individual verses and even entire chapters almost every day. From sixth to eighth grade, Edgar sang in the church choir every Sunday, as well. He fondly remembers praying in the morning and attending church services on Sunday with his parents and younger brother. By the time Edgar finished high school, he was already taking classes at the California State University in Fullerton, where he earned a psychology bachelor's degree at a young age. Then, at age 20, he got sick with ulcerative colitis, interrupting his studies to obtain his master's in psychology. It was then, in the throes of a prolonged gastrointestinal illness, that Edgar decided to become a physician, as "the way I treat other people is the way I treat God, because God is in every person."

Edgar returned to Peru and enrolled in an undergraduate private medical school. For three years, during breaks and vacation periods from school, Edgar undertook fully-supervised training as a medical student in my office for three years. Indeed, he was in the office with me every day, from Monday to Saturday as my assistant, seeing patients with their consent, taking each patient's medical information, giving slide presentations, and learning how to diagnose and treat the most common medical conditions seen in our office. He then transferred to a medical school in Anguilla, where he studied basic sciences for two years. At the time of this writing, he is ready to begin his clinical rotations in some of the hospitals in Chicago, his medical school headquarters, to become a doctor in about two more years.

Edgar has learned to live with and maintain his chronic ulcerative colitis. He has an avid curiosity, a love for learning, and a desire to improve his mind and body keeping through diet and exercise. He still likes to meditate and "learn about [himself]." "All healing comes from within," he says. I have no doubt he will become a most competent physician with a uniquely sensitive disposition, for the very reason he chose the field was to help others who have suffered as he has. I must say it is most gratifying to know that there are still people like Edgar, willing to follow their dreams to become what they are called to be.

Patricia graduated Magna Cum Laude as Bachelor of Science in Nursing in 2013, and Magna Cum Laude with a Bachelor of Science in Medicine in 2017 at the best institution of Manila—the University of Santo Tomas. She came highly recommended to me by Dulce, so I offered her a road map to fulfill her dream of being accepted into a renowned internal medicine residency program in California. The plan involved the hands-on experience of seeing patients with me three days per week, one-on-one teaching, attendance to the CME weekly conferences, oral dissertations, writing a cardiology review article with me, and learning conversational medical Spanish.

From the very start, I realized Patricia had solid knowledge of the medical situations we see in my office. Indeed, after just a few weeks, she was able to practice adult medicine and handle the common cardiology conditions with little supervision on my part. As time went by, she became a sharp young clinician, able to arrive easily at the primary and differential diagnoses as well as confirm them by ordering pertinent tests and prescribing appropriate treatments, following current medical guidelines. Together, we were able to finish the cardiology review article in about six months, and she remained actively engaged in learning Spanish. The fact that she was a nurse before she became a doctor seemed to endow her with a special compassion for each patient she encountered in our office. Her respectful and pleasant personality placed patients and staff alike at ease.

On account of the uncommon potential for professional growth I identified in Patricia, I endorsed her zealously, writing letters of recommendation to several internal medicine residency program directors in September of 2019, as she began her interviews across the nation. I am happy to report that she was accepted and began her residency in a large hospital affiliated with the University of California, San Francisco, in June 2020.

It has been heartwarming for me to meet and contribute to the educational journeys of these and other students who have shadowed me over the years. As one of them wrote to me: *There is some information that cannot be taught in medical school, and that is compassion and love for patients. I very much enjoyed the time I spent with you because it did not feel like work. Shadowing you was such an honor, and has driven me to follow in your footsteps of being a dedicated and hardworking doctor.*

For a humble man, it is terribly flattering to hear these things, but that, of course, is not what motivates me to mentor young doctors. Providing a helpful hand in the education of primary care providers (PCP) is beneficial from every point of view: young physicians are able to better acquaint themselves with the trade in a professional and supportive environment, I am able to express my love of teaching and keep my own skills sharpened, and future patients will benefit from the experience and knowledge acquired by these bright PCPs. From my earliest memorable years, I have felt a calling to serve those who would be helped. This began in the form of teaching math problems to my childhood friends. Today it manifests in both the practice and teaching of medicine. The spiritual rewards for realizing one's calling are infinite; thus, I encourage everyone to pursue his or her own God-given passions with courage and tenacity.

Brain Tumors

In the same way, I am sure, that many of the more enjoyable aspects of running our medical practice go unseen by our patients, there are many invisible rigors with which my staff and I must contend behind the scenes. Resolving these challenges often requires tremendous amounts of work and can at times feel like a business unto itself. There is the crucial business of playing doctor to my patients, and then the matter of maintaining a business and all the daunting complexities therein. And though the rewards of the former will always outweigh the vexations latter, I must admit there have been times when I have felt quite close to a point of submission. It is remembering my love for my patients and the field of medicine that each time allows me to persevere.

But what are these challenges? you may wonder.

Many, I am sorry to say, stem from the medical landscape in this country, which remains in a constant state of flux. Long gone is the era in which a physician could focus solely on what was best for his or her patients, free from the interference of greedy third parties for whom profit is paramount. Now we must often engage in tiresome quarrels with insurance companies, in order to receive authorizations to perform much-needed tests or treatments on our patients. Stacks of paperwork and long questionnaires, however meticulously completed, may still result in a denial of services. This can be truly frustrating for providers working in the best interests of their patients.

Additional complications result from the ways in which health-care plans are structured. Health Maintenance Organization (HMO) plans, for example, form contracts with a set amount of doctors and hospitals in a given area. Members are forced to select their Primary Care Physician (PCP) from this limited pool of local doctors. Their managed care plans are subject to change, and if this occurs, patients may no longer be able to stay with the same physician. HMOs come at lower premiums than other plans, but limit patients' choices and charge them for any healthcare services received from out-of-network providers. Preferred Providers Organizations (PPOs) also provide challenges to both patients and PCPs, requiring providers to contact them to debate the necessity for diagnostic testing in order to obtain authorization in advance of conducting such tests. For radiologic image studies, such as MRIs and CT scans, the process of receiving authorization is even more complicated and may end in disapproval, if the highly specific indications of the health plan are not precisely met.

Regrettably, obtaining authorizations for diagnostics and treatments is not always the end of the battle. Medicare, HMOs, PPOs, and Medicaid periodically conduct audits through which they may later request reimbursement for payments on services that, in the opinion of reviewers, were not medically necessary. The appeal process by which a provider may dispute these rulings is arduous and financially burdensome. At present, there is a backlog of nearly 500,000 Medicare cases awaiting judgment.

It is not my intent to spew an indictment of the healthcare system, nor tout the strength of my resolve as a provider who must abide its many perplexities. What I would offer instead is hope. The fact is the system has not always been this way, and once functioned quite well in a climate focused more on patient care and less on profitability. It is my earnest hope that we will return to a similar system. In the meantime, the best one can do is persevere.

The nature of any difficulty is, of course, relative, as I am routinely reminded when treating patients with complaints of a life-changing nature. It is for them most of all that the trifles of running a medical practice must be set aside, and the business of being an effective physician takes center stage.

I think now of my patient *Anthony*. At 64-years-old, Anthony, a pastor, decided to attend a weekend Christian retreat with his wife, in January of 2007. The first sign of trouble came on the first day of the retreat, when Anthony became confused and picked up the suitcase of another retreat participant, then got dressed in the stranger's clothes. The other retreatant realized what had taken place, and arranged to swap baggage with Anthony, so both men would have their proper belongings. That evening, Anthony's wife was compelled to ask him why he had put on another man's clothes, reasoning that, while it is one thing to mistake a suitcase, it is quite another thing to believe its contents are one's own. Anthony has no explanation for his wife. Later, he began to complain of dizziness and occasional visual difficulties, like the room "going black."

Two weeks after returning from the retreat, Anthony took the wrong freeway to Church. After his wife pointed out his error, Anthony changed course and the couple were able to arrive on time for services, but his wife's concern for him deepened, as this was very unusual behavior for him.

Anthony grew up in a Christian family and began reading the Bible at age 12. He held a full-time job for many years, until his retirement at age 63. For the last 10 years of his career, he also served as a pastor at a congregation, working with his wife on Tuesdays, Thursdays, and weekends, in an impoverished neighborhood. Anthony firmly believed that a good minister should not preach for more than 25 minutes, as anything longer will prevent people from paying attention and receiving the intended message. One day, to the shock of his congregation, Anthony went on preaching for more than 50 minutes, citing Bible quotations without correlation with the topic of his sermon. He then needed to be reminded more than once to bless the bread and wine for the Holy Supper of the congregation. He further struggled to find in his Bible the passage of 1 Corinthians 11: 23-26, regarding the Institution of the Eucharist— a passage he had always known very well.

Lately, he was very concerned and upset because as a Pastor he had to denounce to the police that a man of his flock was sleeping with his wife and his stepdaughter living under the same roof. This was a very sinful situation that made him sad and sick. When his wife came with him to my office following this event, my initial impression was that Anthony was probably suffering from depression, since the neurological and mini-mental state examinations were unremarkable. His wife, however, reported witnessing confusion, memory loss and personality changes in Anthony. Therefore, under the vehement counsel of his wife, I ordered a brain MRI. Anthony did not want to have this test performed, but agreed after some urging, pointing at his head and stating, "I am sure there is only brain, skull and hair here."

A few days later, Anthony's MRI revealed the presence of four brain tumors, with the biggest in the right frontal lobe. Unfortunately, he had a glioblastoma, the most common, aggressive, and highly infiltrative primary malignant tumor, spreading into other parts of the brain. He was seen by the best specialists at Cedars-Sinai Medical Center, and the diagnosis was confirmed by tissue biopsy. At the time,

Anthony was not a candidate for surgery. Thus, he received 35 radiation sessions and chemotherapy. Two months later, a follow-up MRI revealed reduction in tumor size. He subsequently developed various complications associated with his palliative treatment, requiring several hospitalizations.

Despite the gloomy prognosis, Anthony's wife and two sons kept praying and hoping for a miracle. His oldest son was also a minister and evangelist involved in missions in Latin America. He was convinced that his father would overcome the illness with God's help. On more than one occasion, he and I had the opportunity to pray for his father over the phone. Anthony's wife offered the following daily prayer: "Thank you, Lord, for this day. He is in your hands. You can cure him if you want. But, not my will, but your will be done. Amen." Every day, Anthony's wife tended to his personal hygiene, dressing, feeding, and other needs. Every day he remained alive was a blessing to Anthony's family.

Then, one morning in early June 2007, as Anthony was talking to his wife at home, he became confused and unresponsive. Paramedics were called to the scene, and he was taken to the closest emergency department. When his sons were called, they assured their mother that this was just another rush to the hospital, and that Anthony would be fine—no cause for alarm. Sadly, it was not so. After multiple attempts to revive Anthony, he died with his family by his side.

I had the opportunity to attend his funeral along with his family, mother and older sister, a minister as well. Anthony lived with his wife and youngest son, who holds a degree in theology. Over the last 13 years, it has been very difficult for this youngest son to overcome the loss of his father. Nonetheless, he has gradually learned to cope, and is now married and the proud father of an 8-year old girl.

I am glad to report that not all patients with brain tumors succumb to their illness. Indeed, I have had a handful of patients with benign brain tumors who are still alive. *Ian* is one of them. Ian has a long history of diabetes mellitus, hypertension, hyperlipidemia, gastric bypass surgery, heart disease, irregular heartbeats, and other medical conditions. He suffered from meningioma, a tumor that arises from the membranes that surround the brain and spinal cord. Although not technically a brain tumor, it is included as a brain tumor because it may compress the adjacent brain, nerves, and vessels. Meningioma is the most common type of tumor that forms in the head.

By 2017, Ian was 77 years-old, and his symptomatic meningioma in the right frontal and temporal lobes had increased in size up to 5cm. Seven months later, he underwent a successful removal of his meningioma, without major complications or neurological sequelae. In addition, two years later, he undertook removal of the right frontal bone, due to chronic sinus infection and abscess formation. He is now 80 years-old, married, and able to perform activities of daily living by himself.

Perseverance is a necessary component to the survival of any patient who receives a potentially life-threatening diagnosis. The sheer will to fight on exhibited by such patients, in conjunction with my desire to continue administering to them, motivates me to carry on fighting my own comparatively trivial battles. The tribulations of running a medical practice, after all, will never exceed the joys.

> *"So let us not grow weary in doing what is right, for we will reap a harvest time, if we do not give up."— Galatians 6:9*

Heart Attacks

Having now spent roughly four decades in the field of cardiology, I have been immensely fortunate to witness firsthand the incredible evolution of the discipline over the years. I have read with great excitement articles outlining new treatments, medications, and technologies that would go on to save countless lives over the decades. Conditions that at the start of my career might have been labeled death sentences are today controllable with an ever-improving array of medications and cardiac procedures. Surgical and non-surgical techniques have matured from somewhat crude to incredibly sophisticated, commensurate with our expanding knowledge of the heart.

The field of cardiology consists of two main branches: non-invasive and interventional. Non-invasive cardiologists focus on the detection and treatment of heart disease, using external tests—rather than instruments inserted into the body—to evaluate and diagnose cardiac disorders. They rely on tests such as electrocardiograms (EKGs), echocardiograms (heart ultrasound), and stress echocardiograms to perform diagnoses. Interventional cardiologists, by contrast, specialize in the use of catheters—small, flexible tubes that are inserted in the body to repair damaged or weakened blood vessels, narrowed arteries, or other parts of the structure of the heart, such as the valves. Angioplasties with stent deployment are an example of an interventional cardiology procedure. As an interventional cardiologist myself whose office is equipped to perform non-invasive testing, I have been especially fortunate to have had the opportunity to confer the benefits of breakthroughs in both branches of cardiology to my patients.

If you were to ask a stranger on the street to name one medical event or condition associated with the heart, the response you would likely receive is "heart attack"—and this is for good reason. In the United States, someone has a heart attack every 40 seconds. This is a staggering figure, to be sure, but it does not necessarily mean that deaths are occurring every 40 seconds. In fact, today we are so well-equipped to deal with heart attacks that they are rarely fatal. Nonetheless, there remains an urgent need for better education with respect to diet, exercise, and other preventative measures. I work diligently to advise my patients on how to live healthy lifestyles and avoid making choices that will negatively impact their cardiovascular health.

Of course, many patients come to me with preexisting conditions that cannot be controlled with mere diet and exercise. Some present in states that some years ago would have been most dire. I am happy to report that a combination of the aforementioned breakthroughs, prayer, and perhaps sheer will to carry on have resulted in positive outcomes for a great many of them.

I think now of *Edward*, who had complained of chest discomfort for a week before visiting the emergency room. By then he had severe chest pain and shortness of breath. An electrocardiogram revealed the presence of an acute heart attack. He immediately received medical therapy and was transferred by ambulance to another hospital for an urgent angiography of the coronary arteries, which supply blood to the heart.

He was found to have total occlusion of the artery in front of his heart. The artery was opened by using a tiny balloon (angioplasty), with the deployment of a flexible tube made of wire mesh (stent) that remains in place, holding the artery open. This procedure immediately restored the blood flow in the artery, avoiding heart muscle damage due to lack of oxygen.

70-year-old Edward had all of the so-called risk factors—high blood glucose, high blood pressure, high cholesterol, male sex, and age—to develop hardening of the coronary arteries, the most common type of heart disease, killing more than 365,000 people in 2017 in the United States. Two years later, Edward underwent a similar procedure in another coronary artery. He is currently doing well, taking his medications and living with a normal heart function.

Julie was in her early sixties when she first experienced recurrent chest discomfort (angina pectoris) with marked limitations in her activities of daily living. She was treated by two different cardiologists. It was her father, my patient, who proposed to Julie to come to see me, for which she is very grateful until this day. However, in her first office encounter she did not mention her previous heart specialists because "she wanted to see for herself if I will diagnose and correctly treat her heart disease."

"I have always trusted God," she says. Indeed, she has had very difficult experiences to overcome, and she has grown in her faith and love for Jesus. So, "I have always asked the Lord to give you wisdom and use you as his vehicle in ways you can find the best treatment to alleviate my medical conditions. Every time that I went to the cardiac lab, I placed myself in God's hands, asking forgiveness for my sins, and his blessings upon you to use you as his instrument of healing. Therefore, I have faith in God and confidence in you."

Julie suffered her first heart attack at the age of 66. As she was walking in the mall with her husband, she experienced shortness of breath, nausea, and left side jaw pain. She came to my office the next day. From there, she was taken to the cardiac catheterization lab, opening the critical occlusion of her right coronary artery with no residual blockage afterwards.

Julie is the only person in a family of 8 siblings with no history of risk factors for heart disease, other than high cholesterol. Subsequently, she developed more chest pain episodes even at rest, despite optimal medical therapy, prompting repeated hospitalizations with deployment of more stents. Seven years later, in 2014, she underwent a coronary artery bypass grafting surgery.

Now, at 78, Julie is free of angina pectoris, on medical therapy, and with a normal heart function.

It was a Sunday morning, three days before Thanksgiving, when *Joe* got up experiencing severe angina radiated to his left arm. He was 42-years-old, with no previous history of heart disease and in no medications. His entire family, from his maternal grandmother, his parents, wife, and even his children has been my patients since 1994. I went to see him at the emergency department of a local hospital without cardiac catheterization capabilities and arranged his immediate transfer to another hospital because of -most likely- an acute heart attack involving the front artery of his heart.

Indeed, he had a subtotal stenosis in the middle of this artery, which was successfully opened followed by full restoration of the coronary blood flow. His recovery was unremarkable. He stated that, this experience was a close call for him to take better care of himself, lose weight, get nearer to Jesus, and deal better with the always present stress at work and at home.

I am inclined to mention that there have been multiple octogenarian patients in my practice who had severe blockages in all the three coronary arteries, not associated with a heart attack, in whom we were

able to open the three arteries in one single procedure or in two sessions, avoiding to perform coronary artery bypass grafting surgery as
it was their preference.

Because of the presence of metal stents, these patients have to
take medications that make the blood thinner, preventing the formation of clots in the openings of the coronary arteries. The downside is
that a premature discontinuation of this medication or a valid medical
indication to hold it for a few days may result in complications including a heart attack.

In *Caritas in Veritate,* the last of Pope Benedict XVI's encyclicals,
he states that "Technology enables us to exercise dominion over matter, to reduce risks, to save labor, to improve our conditions of life. It
touches the heart of the vocation of human labor: in technology, seen
as the product of his genius, man recognizes himself and forges his
own humanity." In the field of medicine, this is realized through a
beautiful cycle in which the painstaking work of brilliant engineers,
chemists, and other medical scientists gives rise to innovative mech-
anisms for practitioners to better address the needs of their patients.
It is a magnificent example of stewardship, and one in which I shall
forever be honored to play a small role.

End of Living

We come now to the present day and the final chapter—an end of sorts. And though we tend to look upon endings with a certain sadness, it need not always be so, for so often the conclusion of one chapter is but the start of another one greater still. This perspective can be applied to everything from the smallest details in life to the very matter of life itself. One need only look forward.

"I'm very happy. I'm ready to die, but look at me: I have two hands, two feet, and I'm able to speak—I'm fine. I don't want people to feel sorry for me. I'm happy and positive about life. I want to be a bearer of good news and help others with a smile, a good handshake, and a loving hug." That is what *Mike* told me at age 65.

Mike had a long history of heart disease, with triple coronary bypass grafting surgery performed in September of 2011. He underwent two more cardiac procedures—one with the deployment of stents in the native coronary arteries, and one of the grafts in 2019. He suffered another heart attack in between these procedures.

Around the same time, Mike was diagnosed with advanced prostate cancer. He was found to have very large bulging pouches in the terminal segments of the colon, known as diverticulosis. They became inflamed and infected (diverticulitis), which caused him severe abdominal pain, fever, nausea and constipation or diarrhea. By early 2020, his condition had worsened. On one occasion, he had such severe abdominal pain with chills and fever that he became unconscious for three days before going to the hospital. Because Mike was a very high-risk candidate for abdominal surgery, he refused it. He then developed cancer of the pancreas head with multiple metastases to the liver, confirmed by biopsy. This was complicated with obstruction of the common bile duct, which moves the bile from the liver and gall-bladder into the small intestine, where it helps digest the fats in food.

Mike was treated by very competent specialists, but in reality there was no cure for his illness.

Thus, he received only palliative care. He continued losing weight, and experienced weakness and a lack of energy. Independently, he sought the help of a naturopathic physician, who recommended taking a variety of nutritional supplements.

In spite of the difficulties Mike is facing, he keeps his regular appointments with me every three weeks, and on every visit he always displays a positive attitude. A look into the history of this courageous man offers some insight into the origins of his admirable character.

Mike was born near San Francisco in 1954. He has no memory of his father, who abandoned the family when Mike was about three years old. The middle sibling among three, Mike had an older brother and a younger sister. Mike's single mother did her best to support her family, but they were always short on money, and frequently relocated around California.

In elementary school, Mike attended Catechism of the Catholic Church classes in a nearby parish, where, later on as an adult mentor, he would harness his own experience to help children develop good Christian habits and avoid drugs and alcohol.

Mike attended at least five different high schools, and was bullied by his classmates. He never graduated from school or read an English book. Indeed, he left school unable to read. Later, past the age of 30, he realized his illiteracy, taught himself how to read, and obtained a high school diploma. He proudly presented his diploma to his equally proud mother.

According to Mike, he became an "emancipated minor" at age 14. The process of emancipation is a way for children to legally gain adult status before the age of 18. The parents of an emancipated child no longer have legal custody or control over the child. As such, Mike lived in an apartment with several roommates, and worked in whatever job he could find: a gas station, restaurant, landscaping, and security guard—sometimes several concurrently. For example, Mike would work as a security guard from 7pm–7am, sleep a few hours, and then begin work at a gas station. There is no doubt that he worked very hard. He continued to be bullied at school for his short stature, but was physically strong and fought back. His school attendance was far from perfect, but he was not expelled, because he proved to school commissioners that he was working hard and earning a living. In time, Mike would save enough money to rent a house with several friends.

After obtaining his high school diploma in his thirties, Mike studied and obtained a pilot license, flying small seaplanes on deliveries in Seattle. Then he obtained his real estate broker license in California, and opened his own realty company in 1994. Since then he has also taught about moral responsibility, becoming a mentor instructor and advising young men on how to become responsible adults in the military.

Mike says that his life went from crisis to crisis, as he took care of his mom and sister for many years. He was never married, but he had girlfriends for 5 to 8 years duration, one at the time. He states that his relationship with God, Jesus, and nature has grown over the years. He reads Scripture and has a one-to-one relationship with Jesus. "I conduct myself as a Christian gentleman, leading by example, making good choices for myself, and helping others in every way I can."

One of Mike's neighbors is a lady with a 24-year-old son who has been quadriplegic and unable to speak for 22 years. He has helped this young gentleman and his mother for more than 12 years, without expecting anything in return. Mike has cultivated many good friends who mutually help each other whatever the need arises. Recently, an 80-year-old friend called him because of severe chest pain. Mike took the man to the hospital right away. The friend suffered a heart attack. Mike was happy to take care of his friend and the dog he had left behind at home, as he conducts himself as a good Christian with moral values of high standards.

Mike has come to accept his medical conditions and terminal cancer as is. He has complied with all his doctors' appointments, followed their recommendations, and taken his pain medications as needed. He likes to pray at the end of the day. He thinks that God checks on him every night. "I have silent conversations with Jesus, and I repeat positive affirmations aloud to Him" he has told me. "I will be fine, Dr. Caceres. Do not worry. You have been my angel. You are on my shoulder with me at all times. I do not mind driving 35 miles to see you. I appreciate your time and your kindness. I am not a saint. I am a simple man who had received the extra gift to be still around. What else can I ask? Please, pray for me every day as I prayed for you."

And that is Mike—a man who did the ordinary small things at home and at work every day with love. A man who lives with a positive attitude, trying to spread love with his smile and kind words everywhere he goes. He is a man truly unafraid of death, a man prepared for the moment when he is called to eternal life by his Creator.

It is faith that motivates Mike to live in joy, to spread that joy, and to welcome what will ultimately become of him. Mike's life reveals his belief in the resurrection of Jesus Christ, not only through the promise of eternal life after death, but as a reflection of God's plan for humankind. In John 10:10, Jesus says, "I came that they may have life, and have it abundantly." This abundant life, from the most literal perspective, implies longevity and perhaps material prosperity, but the true fullness—and indeed beauty—of a life is realized through suffering, just the same. It is rooted in the formation of our relationship to God, and matures as we live responsible lives in accordance with His plans for us. For Mike, who has faced many challenges in his life and known much suffering, his strong relationship with God renders it no great challenge to remain cheerful nonetheless. Moreover, the spreading of this joyousness to his fellow brothers and sisters is central to his life. And as this full and gracious life comes to an end, Mike feels neither fear nor sadness, but looks ahead to the next beautiful chapter with our God in heaven.

...so that everyone who believes in him may not perish but may have eternal life. — John 3:16

Epilogue

When I began to lay out the groundwork for this book in 2017, I could hardly have imagined how very different the world would look as the work drew to a close in 2020. How shocked I would have been if I could have peered but three years ahead, to see a future of faceless men, women, and children trying to go about their lives in the midst of a frightening pandemic. Add to this political instability, social unrest, and scores of natural disasters and the picture would be most bleak indeed. Yet as I write now in the midst of such uncertainty, I do not fear the future; in fact, I look forward to it.

By now, I expect the secret to my optimism is not so secret. It is, of course, from my faith that I derive a sense of hopefulness, even in the most dismal times.

It is not a question of having sufficient faith to outweigh the gravity of the situations one is facing. Rather, it is a matter of embracing all the matters in one's life—both positive and negative—with a faithful heart. Establishing a strong and authentic relationship with God has enabled me to experience life through the filter of His love. In this way, I am not compelled to distinguish between good experiences and bad experiences with respect to my faith. When I am saddened or feeling lost, I am uplifted by God's love, and when I am joyous, I celebrate the beauty of life with deeper appreciation.

Building and maintaining a close bond with God requires work, of course, but it is so gratifying a journey that it does not feel the slightest bit toilsome. I do not, for example, regard my early morning prayers and Bible reflections as chores I must get out of the way before proceeding with my day. I look upon this morning ritual instead as an opportunity to reconnect with God each day, to show gratitude for the life He has given me, to share with Him my joys and struggles, and to reaffirm my intention to be my best possible self. I quite look forward to this routine, which takes very little time to perform, but confers immeasurable benefits on me, by centering and preparing me for whatever might lie ahead each day.

Does this result in a life without discomfort and apprehension? Certainly not. Like all of God's children, I am susceptible to pain, suffering, and self-doubt. It is important to remember that such sorrows are inescapable aspects of life. It is how one processes the difficulties of life that is most important, and faith offers the most powerful tools for healing available to us. Trust me—I'm a doctor.

In the preceding pages, I provided an account of the ways in which faith informed my life from a child in Peru through my career as a medical doctor in the United States. But that is merely *my* story. You need not be a doctor to benefit from the power of faith. The beauty of the gift of faith is that it is available to us all, whatever one's race, gender, vocation, and denomination. It is an indelible, God-given source of guidance, inspiration, support, and strength, if one but finds the courage to embrace and cultivate it.

And so I encourage you to go forth and write the chapters of your own lives, to remember the value of hard work, to embrace what challenges may come, to be undaunted by uncertainty, and to hold firm to your convictions.

And above all, have *faith*.